Welcome Home

Welcome Home

A Guide to Building a Home
for Your Soul

Najwa Zebian

HARMONY
BOOKS

Harmony
New York

Library of Congress Cataloging-in-Publication Data
Names: Zebian, Najwa, author.
Title: Welcome home / Najwa Zebian.
Description: First edition. | New York : Harmony Books, [2021] |
Includes index.
Identifiers: LCCN 2020054754 (print) | LCCN 2020054755 (ebook) |
ISBN 9780593231753 (trade paperback) | ISBN 9780593231760 (ebook)
Subjects: LCSH: Zebian, Najwa—Dwellings. | Home. |
Self-actualization (Psychology) | Muslim women authors—
Canada—Biography. | Lebanese—Canada—Biography.
Classification: LCC HQ734 .Z435 2021 (print) | LCC HQ734 (ebook) |
DDC 305.48/697071—dc23
LC record available at https://lccn.loc.gov/2020054754
LC ebook record available at https://lccn.loc.gov/2020054755

ISBN 978-0-593-23175-3
Ebook ISBN 978-0-593-23176-0

Printed in the United States of America

Poems from *Nectar of Pain* copyright © 2018 by Najwa Zebian,
reprinted with permission by Andrews McMeel Publishing.

Poems from *Sparks of Phoenix* copyright © 2019 by Najwa Zebian,
reprinted with permission by Andrews McMeel Publishing.

Excerpt from "Scream," *When You Ask Me Where I'm Going* by Jasmin Kaur,
copyright © 2019 by Jasmin Kaur, reprinted with permission by HarperCollins.

Editor: Donna Loffredo
Designers: Meighan Cavanaugh
Illustrator: Meighan Cavanaugh; illustrations based on
original illustrations by Sammy Orlowski
Production Editor: Terry Deal
Production Manager: Jessica Heim
Copy Editor: Mary Anne Stewart
Indexer: Elise Hess
Typeface: PS Fournier, © Stéphane Elbaz, Typofonderie

7 9 10 8 6

First Edition

To every soul in search of a home,

you've reached your destination

Contents

Prologue

I don't know the exact reason you're here. Or why you are holding this book in your hands. So many roads could have led you to this moment. Something tells me you're feeling lost. Isolated. That you are in need of being seen, heard, and loved. That you are in need of feeling safe. Something tells me you've been searching for this state of being in someone other than yourself. Somewhere outside of your own life. Here's the truth: Your home belongs nowhere outside of you. Your home is within you. You are the architect. You are the builder. And you are the occupant. You must find yourself. You must see yourself. Hear yourself. Love yourself. You must create safety for yourself. I know how hard it is to imagine this construction. That's why, in this book, I will hold your hand and guide you as you build your own home within and say to yourself *Welcome home.*

The Road to Home

∽

Before you start building your home, you must lay the brick road that leads to the land on which your home will be built. By breaking down all the obstacles in your way, you will turn your roadblocks into bricks that form the construction of the road.

The mistake most of us make is that we build our homes in other people in the hope that they will deem us worthy of being welcomed inside. We feel so abandoned and empty when people leave, because we've invested so much of ourselves in them. In this introduction, you'll learn about the power of taking ownership over building your home, your own space, within yourself. Regardless of your past, how homeless you were, or how many people you begged to love you, building your home begins here and now.

Are you ready?

Let's start constructing the road to home.

∽

I t was a Monday morning.

I woke up to a message that said "Can I call you?" This was a little unusual for Noah to ask, because we usually planned our calls days in advance. It didn't sit right with me, but since we'd been texting a lot more recently, I decided a phone call was a natural progression. So I answered "Of course!" I jumped out of bed, threw my hair up in a bun, and sat at the island in my kitchen, where I spend much of my time writing.

He called me on his way to work. We talked about his job for a little bit. We laughed a lot. I don't remember why. But I was always very giddy with him on the phone. I liked to make him laugh, even if it meant making a fool of myself.

As we chatted about random life things, something in my heart said *This can't be it. He's calling to tell me something.*

Does he want to find out when he can see me next? Does he want to start opening up more? Does he miss me? No . . . that can't be it. He's so emotionally independent. He would never admit that even if it were true.

But another voice, one that I'd been working so hard on listening to, said *He just wants to talk to you. Relax. You deserve to have someone call you out of the blue just because he wants to hear your voice.*

I listened to that voice this time. It was the same voice I'd listened to a few days earlier when I pushed myself out of my comfort zone and started speaking to him in a more complimentary tone. He wasn't reciprocating every single time, but he was happy to receive the compliments. And at that point, that's all that mattered to me. He was trying to overcome a toxic past, and for him to accept a compliment was a huge step.

I felt happy someone had accepted my praise.

That inner voice took me so far past my comfort zone that I surprised myself. I wasn't used to telling someone how much I wished I could see them. That thought alone—to tell someone I wished I were in their presence—made me blush uncontrollably. I somehow felt ashamed for expressing that . . . for wanting that . . . for admitting that.

You see, in my culture, talking about feelings and romance is taboo. It's only for the movies and TV shows. It's like, as a child, you could watch these shows, but you had to know what happened in them couldn't happen in real life. It was a kind of cognitive dissonance. *That happens and it's okay for others to experience it, but if I did it, I would be in trouble.*

At least that's how I grew up in a tiny village in Lebanon. Everyone was of the Muslim faith—on paper. The mosque was right across from my house. And I grew up with a heavy religious education. That education drew hard lines between girls and boys, men and women. As a child, this is how I saw relationships: One day your knight in shining armor sees you, somehow, even though you're hidden. He says he's in love with you and wants to marry you. And, boom. You live happily ever after.

Ironically, way at the other end of the world—the part of the world where I'd eventually learn how misguided that notion of relationships is—Disney movies taught girls the same thing. I now know this is a narrative springing from misogyny and patriarchy—which unfortunately know no borders—rather than specific religions or cultures. I could write books about this, but let's get back to the voice I was talking about.

Because whenever I listened to that voice, I slept better and felt happier, I decided on this morning to listen to that voice, too.

So I told him how excited I was to see him. Because he was so busy with work, we had decided to meet in a month's time. But that voice had told me a few days before this call that if I wanted to see him sooner, I should just let him know. So I did so in a text message.

He said he would let me know when he could see me within the next week. I thought this was great. I had convinced myself that I needed to be more expressive, because I knew, given his toxic past, which he'd briefly mentioned, he had trust issues. *I'd better make him feel secure with me,* I thought. *I'd better make him feel valued and wanted.*

At the first moment of awkward silence in our phone call, I said: "I know I may have been saying things you're not fully ready to hear, but I hope hearing them reminds you of how valuable you are." Those things I'd said were innocent compliments and affirmations.

And then he said, "That's the thing . . . I don't think we should talk anymore."

Let me freeze this moment for you and explain exactly how I felt: I was shocked. But at the same time, I really wasn't. I knew this moment was coming. I wasn't actually happy with our dynamic. I knew I wasn't happy. In retrospect, I confused the happiness being vulnerable and speaking my mind gave me with him making me happy. But his lack of reciprocation always left me feeling confused. Getting emotion or attention from him was like running a race with the illusion there was a finish line. So you keep running, and the finish line keeps moving farther and farther away from you. Against all the odds of how I thought I would respond, I actually fell quiet. I could feel my body shrink and curve. My oversized sweater felt like the closest thing to a hug I could get during this moment, which felt like it would never end. How could it end when I hadn't even seen it starting? *Of course this would happen to me. No one wants to be with me.*

In this moment of silence, he said: "See, the last few days have been way too intense. I'm not ready for something like this."

Way too intense? I thought. *We were just TEXTING!*

I immediately jumped into defense mode and said: "But you said you were happy."

"I did say that. And I was happy. But it just made me realize that I'm not ready. It's too soon. I'm still dealing with a lot of things from my past, and I have to resolve them on my own."

So the answer was simple. I said: "Okay, I won't talk to you like that anymore. I'm sorry."

But there was that other voice again: *I moved too fast. I said things I shouldn't have said. Maybe if I had waited a little bit longer, things would have been different. This is my fault.*

"I think you're in too deep, and it wouldn't be fair to you to ask you to take a step back. So I think for now the best thing is that we don't talk anymore."

"At all?"

"At all. I know you don't want to hear this, but I'm not going to change my mind. I know this hurts, but that's what I want."

As I attempt to describe this pain, words crumble before they can be written on paper. It felt like someone had walked me all the way up to the top of a mountain and pushed me off with all their force. At the same time, I felt numb. Perhaps it was denial. Shock. Disbelief. Or maybe the pain was so deep I couldn't feel its intensity anymore. I felt a tingling sensation all over my body. Like

I wanted to cry, but I couldn't cry. I wanted to yell, but I couldn't yell. I guess what I really wanted was to change this ending. But I couldn't.

This was the end of the fight.

I felt so helpless.

How do you continue to fight when there's no one but you on the battleground? How do you fight when someone has already raised your white flag for you? How do you say goodbye to someone who's already gone? Who's already left and is just informing you of their departure after they've reached their destination?

The rest of the phone call was a blur.

I took a business meeting immediately afterward, so I had no time to cry. When it ended, I jumped on a call with my business partner at the time and braved through it. But near the end of the call, he asked: "Are you okay?"

Honestly, back then, I resented this part of myself. It's so readily apparent when I'm struggling. You can hear it in my voice. You can see it in my eyes. It's so obvious. I mean, this person on the phone with me sensed something was wrong. The first thing I thought was *Ugh! I hate that I can't even hide how I'm feeling over the phone.*

I said: "Honestly, I'm not okay." And that's when I broke down in tears. I told him what happened.

"I don't understand why this always happens to me . . . it hurts so much . . . my heart actually hurts. I'm going to need to take some time off. I can't focus on the work we agreed on."

He was so kind, and he gave me so much input that, at the time, seemed to go in one ear and out the other. My whole being was preoccupied with this pain. This was bigger than Noah. It quickly spiraled into overblown feelings of abandonment, neglect, and worthlessness.

It was the weirdest thing ever. I said to myself *Why are people always so okay with not having me in their lives?*

I was taking an active part in degrading myself. I was telling myself *Who do you think you are?* I thought I'd already done the internal work to change the answer from *I am a nobody* to *I am Najwa Zebian*. How could it be that the answer was now back to *I am someone who's not worthy of love?*

Somewhere between feeling I was a narcissist for being unable to accept that someone was okay not being with me and knowing what my value was, I chose to listen to a voice that told me *You still don't know how to let people see your value. If you did, this wouldn't have happened.*

So for the next few days I kept going over every moment. Every part of this story with Noah where I messed up. I was going in circles. I mean, this was never even close to a relationship. We didn't even date. It was always a prospect, an *almost*, but never really there. The intensity of the pain I felt was so out of balance with the way I actually felt about Noah. I wasn't in love with Noah. I wasn't even in *like* with Noah. I was in *hope* with Noah's potential. I was hurting more over *someone* leaving than over who that someone was.

My business partner had offered to connect me with his therapist, Brittany. At this point, I hadn't spoken to a therapist in a while because I'd felt I was getting nowhere in therapy. But I decided to give it another try.

After I described my shock to the therapist, this is how the text conversation went:

THERAPIST: First, emotions are energy in motion, meaning that although they seem so hard and real, they truly are just energy that will flow through and which we can absolutely work through. Second, of course it would be a shock, because you probably would have done things a bit differently. Third, it's really our ego that gets hurt in this situation. Sometimes we just want to be the one to make those decisions and be the one to cut the ties.

(It did cross my mind multiple times that if anyone should have ended this communication, it should have been me!)

THERAPIST: So I'd ask, when he stated you two wouldn't be speaking anymore, how does that truly affect who you are and what you are?

ME: I believe it just confirms that I'm not worthy of being held on to. Not because I don't believe I'm not worthy of being held on to. But because every experience in my life up to this point has proved that I'm not.

THERAPIST: Sounds like it wasn't exactly someone you wanted to hold on to you.

ME: I think I wanted to be held on to by him, but not the way he was holding on to me, which implies I wanted to change the way he feels. And I have no power to do that.

THERAPIST: So do you feel it's really him you wish would hold you? Or someone in general?

(Even a therapist I was speaking to for the first time could tell that it wasn't Noah I was sad over.)

ME: I know for sure it's someone in general, but I . . . felt a connection with him. The first time I met him, I saw sorrow. And I felt this pull to try to help him. And every time he opened up and was vulnerable, I felt a stronger and stronger connection with him. I was familiar with that sorrow. It was comfortable to be in the presence of it. Because I understood it so well.

THERAPIST: Sorrow—a thing that you could relate to quite strongly . . . It's a healer thing. When we see others experiencing sorrow, we want to protect them. We want to help them with the pain. We want them to know that they aren't alone. Physically or emotionally. It doesn't matter. It all hurts the same way. The body keeps score. And when those things continually happen, they create strong neuropathways that cause our belief of not being worthy or not good enough to become more and more ingrained. Then when we find someone who has experienced similar pain, it hurts even more when they seem to do the same to us. Such as in this situation when he abruptly said you shouldn't talk anymore and walked away.

After this text exchange, we decided to speak over the phone in three days. The next few days were a blur. I just went with my feelings wherever they took me. I spent so much time wondering why I was hurting over someone I wasn't even close to being in a relationship with. I beat myself up over not being the one to say that we shouldn't speak anymore. I felt something was wrong with me for having what felt like an overblown reaction to a slightly significant event.

When I finally spoke with my therapist on the phone, she said something that made me cry uncontrollably for the rest of the day: "Something is telling me that you experienced something in the past that shaped your belief of lack of self-worth."

It literally felt like I had poison, electricity, or pain rushing through my veins—a wound inside of me was all of a sudden open and gushing all over my body, looking for an exit. An escape.

Talking to this therapist made me realize that the reason I was getting nowhere was that at that time, in my late twenties, I had fallen into the trap most of us fall into—the trap of continuing to talk about my *current* pains, convincing myself that just talking about them, giving them a voice and validating them, was enough to resolve them. A hurricane of emotions ripped through my body as I reached for a tissue.

The irony was, I knew the harsh truth. I had discussed it in my many speaking engagements and had shared it with my million-plus social media followers: You can heal a recent wound, but if you haven't come to terms with your past wounds, you can be sure those wounds will turn into scars that will continue to define you.

Until that day, I had always believed the scar I bear—the one that served to remind me I was unworthy—was not having a consistent sense of home during my younger years. I grew up in Lebanon. I was the youngest in my family, with a considerable age difference between me and the rest of my siblings. One after the other, they made their way back to Canada, where they were born. I lived with different relatives and always felt disconnected and out of place. Even when I lived at home, the age gap between me and my siblings, and between me and my parents, made the connection harder. This scar was made worse when a summer trip to visit my family in Canada at sixteen unexpectedly turned into a permanent stay. That dislocation had been jarring, and though Canada was a welcoming place, I still felt homeless. Now, as I reached for the whole damn box of tissues, I realized my scars had actually formed years earlier. Noah was nothing more than a trigger—one that led me to wonder about the source of my pain.

I don't remember the exact date, but I was around eight or nine years old, staying at my aunt's house. My mom was in Canada at the time and my dad had work and thought that I'd be better taken care of with my aunt. It was the night before Eid, a major Muslim celebration. My aunt came and asked her kids to go downstairs. She told me to stay where I was, because this was "our family time." Meaning the family did not include me.

I was left alone in the empty room upstairs, staring at the metal fireplace in front of me. I could hear my cousins opening gifts, their laughter pouring through the walls. They sounded so happy as they exclaimed "Look what I got!" to one another.

All my heart could say then was *Why can't I have that?*

That wasn't the gifts. It wasn't the clothes or the candy.

That was the love. The warmth. The connection. The feeling of relevance, worth, and importance. . . . Like I actually belonged somewhere.

At such a young age, I wasn't able to label my feelings with these words. The only word I could put to what I was missing, to what I wanted, was *that*.

Speaking to my therapist, I was telling the story as if it were happening now. But this time, I could finally see why on a theoretical level, I could speak in front of thousands and tell my audience everything there is to know about self-love and worth and not accepting less than what you deserve. But when it came to actually applying it to my life, I was that little girl who believed that she didn't deserve *that*.

When something traumatic happens to us, we look for someone to blame. I couldn't blame anyone for not giving me what I couldn't even name. So who did I blame?

I blamed myself.

I blamed myself for wanting *that*. I blamed myself for not feeling genuine happiness without *that*. I even blamed myself for my ache, my longing, to feel *that*.

Since that age, and up to this day, I've been on my journey to find *that*.

That is home.

Home is not a physical place. It is the place where your soul feels it belongs, where you can unapologetically be yourself, where you are loved for your authentic self. Home is the place where you don't have to work hard just to be loved.

I explained to my therapist how it felt to be left behind, carrying my home in my backpack. My words. My journal. That was the place I went when someone bullied me at school or made fun of me. That was the place I went when I felt like I was aching for *that*.

And I told her how it felt to arrive in Canada, years later. At this point, all my older siblings were also living there, and I was excited to reunite with them for what I thought would be a temporary stay.

I didn't get a chance to say a real goodbye to my home in Lebanon, my room, my grandparents, my friends, and all the places that I knew. For a whole year, I felt invisible. I felt betrayed, and I didn't even know by whom. By life? By war? By fate?

When I became certain I was "stuck" in Canada, I was so angry with myself that I ripped up every single page of the journal I'd been writing in for the past three years. What was the point of expressing myself if no one heard it? What was the point of writing my feelings down if I wasn't able to do anything to change my reality?

I was done with writing. I was done with feeling.

It wasn't until seven years later, at twenty-three, when I was getting my master's degree in education and I started teaching, that something in me changed. The principal walked in with a group of eight refugees, and as I looked at them, their eyes screamed *What am I doing here? I don't belong here.*

All I wanted to scream back was *You do belong here. I know how you feel.*

I started writing to empower them and advocate on their behalf. To write in order to fight for someone else—that was okay. I convinced myself I was writing about them, not myself.

Little did I know that by helping them heal, I was healing my eight-year-old self who was told to stay behind. I was healing my sixteen-year-old self who ripped up her journal and gave up on feeling. Those writings became my first book, which I put out into the world with the hope that it would help one person sitting in that dark corner of life, searching for a home, just like me.

A few months after I'd self-published my first book, *Mind Platter*, a team from TEDxCoventGardenWomen reached out to me, asking me to take the stage. The theme was "It's About Time." I thought to myself, *It's about time to feel.* So I titled my talk "Finding Home Through Poetry."

Fast-forward a few months.

Moments before I walked onto the stage, I took a deep breath and told myself *Forget the script. Say what your heart needs to say.*

I had planned a big speech on how I'd built my own home by writing poetry. I'd been working on memorizing it for the last six months. Sitting in my hotel room the night before, I found myself more focused on memorizing the words in the right order than I was on truly sharing my heart and soul. I was feeling a mix of panic and numbness—panic because how could I not have memorized it when I'd had six months to do so? And numbness because no way was I backing out of this speech. I'd taken a day off from teaching and had spent two thousand dollars just for a forty-eight-hour trip to London and a one-night stay at a hotel room that was so small I could barely breathe in it.

Plus, this was the first time I'd been asked to take the stage to speak to five hundred people. I had to do it. This is, after all, what I wanted. A chance to be heard. A chance to speak for myself.

I put the papers on my bed and decided to go for a walk.

It felt like the night before a big exam. There's no running away from the fact that this is your one and only chance to prove you know what you claim to know—but you're in denial about that. The closer it gets, the less likely you're able to retain any information related to it.

I left my tiny hotel room, still wondering why on earth it was so expensive. I took my phone with me in case I needed directions back to the hotel. This was unusual for me to do. I used to be very afraid of getting lost. *But,* I thought, *I'm going to walk in a straight line anyway.*

About ten minutes after I started walking, I noticed big open gates and crowds of people. I thought *This is so cool!* Back home, you can see like five people on the streets. Lo and behold, what was ahead explained why I had to pay so much for my hotel room.

Buckingham Palace. In all its glory.

I don't know about you, but I believe that every moment we live is connected to all the other moments. Some moments we live now are connected to moments ten or twenty years from now. And we don't see the connection until that future moment happens. And it's kind of like an *ah-ha* moment when you say, "Now I understand why that moment in the past happened." It's like a sweet trick of the universe. Sometimes these are moments of closure. Sometimes they're moments of new beginnings. Sometimes they're moments of deeper understanding of oneself. Sometimes they're just moments of relief. And this moment here was one that, two years later, I could fully understand the meaning of.

Let's go back to Buckingham Palace. I was never the type to be blown away by glamorous looks or riches, but I loved the design, the architecture. I also loved seeing people taking pictures and enjoying themselves. As I watched, I remembered a moment from my childhood. I remembered a small ripped piece of paper that I'd kept in my journal. It was a picture of a beautiful princess in a wedding dress that had the longest train I'd ever seen. Next to the picture was written in Arabic something to the effect of "She died in a car crash in Paris."

That's all I knew. I remember keeping that picture because I thought she was so beautiful. On some level, I wanted to be like her.

Now that I think of it, I was seven years old when that news came out. I kept that picture for a long, long time. As I stared at Buckingham Palace, picturing the footsteps the People's Princess took in its halls, a moment of revelation struck me: It wasn't that I wanted to be like her. My younger self must have felt I shared something with her. That something was the story of search for a home. And there was a reason Princess Diana left a mark in the world: her willingness to show her heart and talk about her real pain. I knew I was meant to go for this walk to get to this exact moment. I knew what I needed to say the next morning.

I walked back to my hotel. With the time difference, I couldn't fall asleep. I needed to be on location at 8:00 a.m. London time, which was 3:00 a.m. at home in Canada. It was brutal. But I woke up at what would have been 1:00 a.m. to get ready and be there on time. I was depleted in every way possible.

I was informed when I arrived that I was the first speaker of the day. The organizer—an incredibly sweet woman—told me that some people, when they found out I was speaking, had begged for there to be an exception to this sold-out event, so they could come and see me speak. I remember her saying "They said: 'We will stand on the sides just to hear her speak.'" That warmed my heart, but there was a voice in my head that said *Oh, she's just being nice. That can't be true.* And even if I allowed myself for a moment to believe it, that voice said *Why would they want to hear* you *speak so badly?*

I don't remember much more about that morning besides having to rehearse part of my speech. Then I went on stage. At one point, the following words, which I didn't plan, left my mouth effortlessly:

The biggest mistake we make is that we build our homes in other people. We build those homes and we decorate them with the love and care and respect that makes us feel safe at the end of the day. We invest in other people, and we evaluate our self-worth based on how much those homes welcome us. But what many don't realize is that when you build your home in other people, you give them the power to make you homeless. When those people walk away, those homes walk away with them, and all of a sudden, we feel empty because everything that we had within us, we put into them. We trusted someone else with pieces of us. The emptiness we feel doesn't mean we have nothing to give, or that we have nothing within us. It's just that we built our home in the wrong place.

Let's fast-forward to the moment Noah said: "I can't do this anymore." Yes, that means I spoke those empowering words *before* my experience with him.

Actually, let's jump ahead again to the moment I told my therapist: "I believe it just confirms for me that I'm not worthy of being held on to. Not because I don't believe that I'm not worthy of being held on to. But because every experience in my life up to this point has proved I'm not."

Let's *dissect this moment*. How could I have helped millions heal with my words but still be that eight-year-old wondering *Why can't I have that?* I knew so much. I could stand on stage and give the best speech on self-love. I could write endlessly about self-worth, empowerment, and value. Why couldn't I actually *feel* it?

There's a problem. Isn't there? And it needs to be solved.

I thought that I'd started building my real home a few years ago, when I'd had all those realizations about building homes in other people.

Clearly, I hadn't.

I did the work—the work of learning. Of researching. Of feeling the pain at every level. In education, we refer to the transfer of knowledge on a theoretical level to a practical level as *praxis*. Where was my praxis? How could I know all this and then go back to being that eight-year-old girl alone in a room saying *Why can't I have that?*

Why can't I have that?

Why *can't* I have that?

Ah-ha. There's one problem.

I fundamentally believed, like the eight-year-old me, that I can't have that.

Can't.

Do you see what the problem is?

The word *can't* automatically states *that* was not achievable. And the only reason it's not achievable is that it wasn't achieved in the past. How ridiculous is that? It's like saying I can't graduate from high school because I haven't graduated from high school before. Or that I can't travel because I haven't traveled before.

You get the point.

So let's change the question from "Why can't I have that" to "Why *don't* I have that?"

Boom.

Now that the question does not imply impossibility, but rather pushes for discovery and understanding, I can actually search for answers.

Why **can't** I have *that*?	Why **don't** I have *that*?
• Implies that *that* is not achievable	• Implies that *that* is achievable
• Strips away your power: "I will never have it."	• Doesn't strip away your power: "I don't have it yet."
• Calls for submission	• Calls for purpose
• Serves as a roadblock	• Serves as a road *brick*

The goal of constructing the road that leads to your home within is not to avoid the roadblocks in your way. Rather, it is to break them down and use them as road *bricks* you can interlock to construct the road. That is what makes the road to your home within unique to you.

The tools in this chapter will help you lay the brick road leading to your home within. Take each roadblock in your way and break it down into bricks. Repeat this with each roadblock you come across. Imagine those bricks being used to construct the road to your home within.

TOOL #1: IDENTIFY YOUR *WHY CAN'T I HAVE THAT?* STORY

Go all the way back to where you started forming the story that you are not worthy of having *that*.

Ask yourself *What does that story make me believe about myself?*

Reflect on all the experiences where you responded or acted from that belief.

TOOL #2: CHANGE THE QUESTION

Using the diagram on the previous page, change your *Why can't I have that?* story to a *Why don't I have that?* story. This tool is essentially a mindset shift. Believe what you're aiming for is achievable.

For the longest time, I believed that I could not have *that*—that I could not have the feeling of home. And, since I'd rendered myself powerless with that belief, it meant I was waiting for someone to build that home for me. That in itself is a problem, but the bigger, more dangerous problem is this: I didn't believe I was worthy of having a home for myself within myself. I was still waiting for someone to give me love. Someone to give me worth. Someone to give me value. I was giving more power to my past lived experience and what I thought it proved than I was giving to my current living experience and what I knew about myself in the present.

On an intellectual level, I knew that building a home for myself was something I needed to do independently of others, but there I was, feeling excruciating pain when someone didn't welcome me into their home, when someone didn't give me love. There I was, working so hard to derive my worth from external sources of validation—people, titles, degrees, acquaintances, social circles, and so on. The feeling of homelessness led me to take any hint of a possibility of a connection, relationship, friendship—BELONGING to anything—as better than being homeless altogether. I lived in dreams and hopes of homes in other people and things more than I actually lived in their homes. When you don't know what home looks like, you take whatever you're offered.

My feeling of homelessness not only made me betray myself while I built homes in others, it also made me betray others by having insincere feelings for them (even though my feelings seemed sincere to me). In reality, I was looking to them as shelters for the scattered pieces of myself more than I was looking at them as people to love.

So this is where I was. At square one of building my own home. I had knowledge of all the elements of self-awareness and self-acceptance, but I hadn't put them together. I hadn't reached praxis. And I hadn't created a place for this knowledge within myself. It's like having a living room, dining room, kitchen, bedroom, and bathroom without having them connected and in one place. Would you say you owned a home if every piece of it were in a different place?

So now I ask you, *Where are you now?*

I mean in your healing. *Where are you now?*

TOOL #3: CONSTRUCT THE ROAD

1. Reflect: *Where am I now?* I'm guessing you're in a state of not feeling home.

2. Reflect: *Where do I want to be?* I'm guessing you want to build a home within you.

3. *What's standing in the way of your getting there?*

    a. Your Why can't I have *that?* story (Tool #1)

    b. Your belief that you *can't* have *that.*

4. Change your mindset (Tool #2).

5. Start making the journey home.

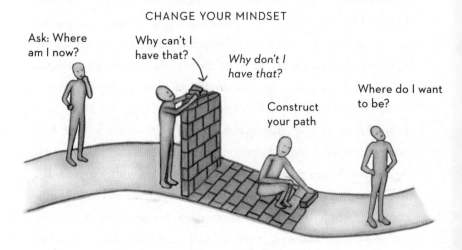

CHANGE YOUR MINDSET

Ask: Where am I now?

Why can't I have that?

Why don't I have that?

Construct your path

Where do I want to be?

On your journey of learning who you are and what feels like home to you, you will have to take an inventory of what's in your life and reflect on what feels like home to you and what doesn't. This will help you find your *third space*. I will explain. Right after completing my bachelor's degree in education, I went on to pursue a master's degree in education in muliliteracies and multilingualism. One of the concepts I learned that stuck with me is the "third space"—the space in which students feel most comfortable expressing themselves. The first space would be their home and the second space would be their school, with all the different identities they have in each. The third space would be that in-between space where they are able to express the mixture of identities they feel represent them the most.

Even though I learned this concept in the context of education, I have adapted it to life in general. We each have our own third space. It's the space in which we feel we are our authentic self. It's the space that contains all our preferences for how we would like to live our life. It's the ideal space in which we feel fully and wholly represented. It's . . . *home*.

I never felt, and still don't feel, like I fully belong in either my first or my second space. I didn't feel that way either before or after age sixteen. Neither the culture I carried with me from Lebanon nor the one I encountered in the West fully represented me on its own. Creating my own third space required my own definition of *freedom*. My own definition of *woman*. My own definition of *home*.

TOOL #4: IDENTIFY YOUR THIRD SPACE

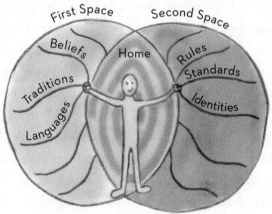

Which parts represent → you?

1. Identify the two spaces or worlds you feel you are living in.
   (Note: There could be more than two. If there are, draw additional circles. The goal is not to get stuck on the term *third*
   space. It's *your space*. Your *home*.)

2. Write down all the required identities, rules (spoken or unspoken), beliefs, languages, traditions, standards, and the like, of
   the spaces you identified in step 1.

3. In your third space, or *your* space, write down the identities,
   rules, beliefs, languages, standards, and the like, that you feel
   represent your authentic self.

Trust me, I know what it feels like to not know where to start. And
this is exactly why I am writing this book. I remember feeling crippled
for so long. Not crippled—chained. I remember feeling stuck. Feeling
I'd been sitting with this pain for so long that it had become my comfort zone, my home. Feeling too afraid to venture beyond it. Because,
at least, this place was safe. It was predictable. And comfortable.

But feeling chained wasn't the worst part. The worst part was
when I realized I had wings, when I'd realized my power but was
still choosing not to fly. To not be free. That is one of the most defeating forms of self-oppression—to know you have power, but not
use it. To know you have a voice, but not speak. To know you are in
the wrong place, but stay where you are. To know you have so much
potential, but not use it. Now that I know my *Why can't I have that?*
story and how it served as a roadblock, I understand why I was de-
terred from building my own home, even after I realized I needed to.

It is my belief that the fear we have of cutting the chain and
breaking free comes from a lack of self-acceptance. It comes from
believing what the roadblocks tell us about ourself. Self-acceptance

tells you that your self-worth is not conditioned by your circumstances. You're worthy no matter what's happening in your life. You may be making excuses about why you're not doing the work of breaking free, but once you accept yourself, you won't be able to buy into them anymore. For example, you might say *If I make this change*:

- They will think of me differently.
- They won't welcome me anymore.
- They won't love me anymore.
- They won't respect me anymore.
- And so on . . .

This necessitates that question Who are *they*? Who is your audience? And why are they the most important? Is your audience from your first space or second space?

TOOL #5: SEE A BIGGER WORLD (AUDIENCE)

One of the things that stops us from taking the journey back to our-selves is our fear of being judged, shamed, or even ostracized from the lives of those around us. When you think of making a change, whose reactions to this change worry you the most? Which peo-ple first come to mind? The people you're afraid of. The people you want to please. The people whose judgment you worry about. You're perceiving those people as giants, aren't you? That's because you're giving them power. They're confining the limits of your world. Now I want you to imagine breaking the confines of that circle and seeing a bigger audience, a bigger world. How freeing is that?

When you limit your ability to break free because you're seeking acceptance from those around you, you're refusing to break down that roadblock and turn it into a road brick. You're failing to build a home for yourself within yourself. You will spend years of your life being fully aware of how much more you deserve but blaming your surroundings for keeping you from choosing to be the leader of your own life.

I spent most of my life searching for *that*, the feeling of home, anywhere but in myself. I always came from a place of emptiness, looking for something or someone to fill that void. That meant that I was always working toward something. That was my full-time, 24/7 job. At various points in my life, that something took different forms. At one point, it was a stage of life that everyone around me reached, like marriage and kids. And a career that would fit with that life. At another point, it was higher grades. A degree. A job. An award that would tell me I was doing great, that I was doing better than others. At another point, it was being included in certain friend circles. The amount of money that I spent on birthday, engagement, and wedding gifts hurts me to think of now. I was always invited to birthday parties and I went even if I didn't know the girl whose party it was that well. I can't remember a single time when someone threw a birthday gathering for me. Yet I continued to accept invites. I stayed in friendships when I knew I was being taken advantage of, because I thought that having part-time friends was better than not having any at all.

Do you remember when I said that I was just happy that Noah was accepting my compliments? This was the same pattern. People accepting what I had to give was all I needed to keep seeking a connection with them. Because that was my audience (the smaller circle in Tool #5). Because that told me that they were welcoming me into their lives. Because their acceptance of what I had to give gave me a temporary feeling of validation that what I had within me was worthy. And it wasn't until I could see this pattern of constantly seeking a home in others that I could see the only consistent home I could ever have is within me.

Once you have built a home within yourself, you are unstoppable. Because you are no longer a walking homeless person begging for someone to give you shelter. You are not standing at every intersection and every corner begging for whatever leftovers or pocket change people have to give you.

And once you've built a home within yourself, you will no longer be in a reactive mode in relation to the world around you. You are not in a state of defining yourself in comparison to others. You're not in a state of feeling good about yourself just because you feel you are "better" than others based on how much money you make, what your job title is, what your social status is, and the like. In a state of at-homeness, you are not constantly knocking on other people's doors, pointing out to them how their actions or words are wrong.

You understand that others may throw rocks at your home, but those rocks don't mean anything about you unless you *make* them mean something about you. You focus on fixing the damage within your home, rather than waiting for the rock-throwers to give you permission to do so by apologizing for what they did. You also don't focus on revenge or throwing rocks back at them.

You are able to see people's actions and words as separate from what you know and believe about yourself.

DON'T FAKE *THAT* TILL YOU HAVE *THAT*

When you find yourself
looking at those around you
wondering
"why can't my life be like that?*"*
or
"why can't I have that?*"*
remember
you don't need anyone's that
to be happy.
You need you
to be happy.
Because your that *is within* you.
And if you can't see you,
you'll never see that.

If your current state is devoid of *that*, you will be working toward your desired state from a place of thirst. From a lack of worth. From a place of trying to prove to yourself that you deserve *that*. Think of a plant. If you want a plant to grow and you keep imagining how beautiful it will look as it grows but you don't give it what it needs the plant's growth will be stunted. There's no point in waiting until you deem the plant beautiful before giving it the care it needs. It will never grow that way. It will never fulfill the potential you know it has.

The same applies to you.

You can't deprive yourself of the belief that you deserve *that* until you look like, feel like, and have the things and people in your life that you believe will make you have *that*.

Do you understand how absolutely essential it is for you to start constructing the road to building your own home within yourself? How beautiful and liberating it would be to have the sense of belonging independent of where you are or who you are with? How beautiful it would be to feel at home wherever you go because that home is within you, not anywhere else?

We'll begin building your home with the foundation. After you've built your home's foundation, you'll have a place for all the parts of yourself to stand and be together on. When you enter any of the rooms to come, remember the foundation on which they lie— your self-acceptance and self-awareness. Not someone else's acceptance of you or knowledge of you.

And when times get rough, as they will, I want to remind you of these words that I wrote in *The Nectar of Pain*:

> *These mountains that you are*
> *carrying,*
> *You were only supposed to*
> *climb.*

These mountains that you are carrying,
you were only supposed to climb.

This is a mantra that I use anytime I feel powerless. These words paved the way for me to save myself by reminding me that nothing thrown my way is meant to drag me down, but is instead an opportunity to learn, to overcome, and to rise above. This mantra helps me through moments of healing, from understanding the simplest of emotions to healing from traumas I carried for years. It also helps me to walk through difficult times. I say it before I go on stage, before interviews, before having a difficult conversation, or when I have a big project that feels like it's too big and I don't know where to start. I say it to remind myself that I am the one in power. Use it as it fits your needs anytime you feel powerless. It applies perfectly to the context of building your home.

The mere visualization of moving that heavy weight from being above you to being below you gives you power. Through the road to your home, the building of the foundation and the rooms, and your entry into each room, you will discover you are carrying mountains of pain, trauma, and rejection; of feeling not good enough, like you feel too much, like you do too little or too much. Whatever it is, remember this: Even though it might feel like these mountains are crushing you and that you are powerless in comparison to them, you are the one with power. You are the one who gets to say *I am putting this mountain beneath my feet and rising above*. And when you reach the top of that mountain, you'll look back and say *Wow! Look how far I've come. And because I conquered this mountain, I can conquer any other mountain that's thrown my way*.

There is no specific order in which you should enter the rooms. Your healing is a personal journey. You are the builder of your own home. You enter the rooms based on what you need. Upon entering certain rooms, you might become aware of your need to enter another one first. As I wrote this book, I ordered the rooms based on how my healing unfolded before my own eyes. As you build your own home, enter and exit the rooms as your healing unfolds before you.

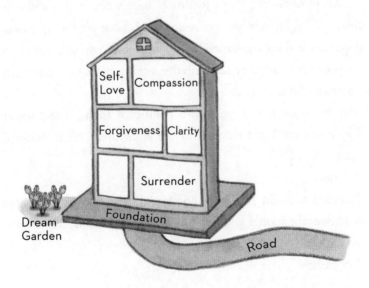

To learn the practice of loving yourself authentically, enter the Self-Love room (Chapter Two).

To learn how to let go and forgive, enter the Forgiveness room (Chapter Three).

To learn about compassion with yourself and others and how to build boundaries, enter the Compassion room (Chapter Four).

To see your authentic self clearly through your own eyes, enter the Clarity room (Chapter Five).

To learn how to drop the resistance against feeling emotions, positive or negative, enter the Surrender room (Chapter Six).

To learn how to discover your passion and live your dreams, enter the Dream Garden (Chapter Seven).

Since listening to yourself is at the core of building your own home, this art is present in every room. The Art of Listening to Yourself (Chapter Eight) will explain the power of this skill in nurturing your at-homeness.

In Adapting to Your New Reality (Chapter Nine), you will consolidate all the knowledge you've acquired about your unique healing journey and the construction of your home. You will learn how to be your new, authentic self with the world around you, especially the people who already know you.

Finally, to customize your own additional room(s) and see an example of how I did so, turn to the appendix, "What Room(s) Would You Add?"

It's time.

It's time to build your own home within yourself. The sooner you do that, the sooner you'll be able to tell yourself *Welcome home*.

Are you with me?

Let's begin.

ONE

Building a Foundation

~

The foundation of your home is its most important part. If there is no foundation, you can have all the elements needed for your home, but the lack of a foundation jeopardizes the control you have over these elements. Without a foundation, you will feel unorganized and chaotic. You'll look to others for stability, putting yourself at risk of defining your worth through external validation.

Many of us rush into learning about all the elements that make us feel like home without seeing the value of the integration of these elements—without learning about the importance of a foundation to pull them together.

The foundation is built from two things: *self-acceptance* (you must feel worthy of the foundation) and *self-awareness* (knowing who you are). Without the foundation, the rooms of your home can't be accessed. A foundation is essential for all the rooms to have a place in your home and to weather the storms that threaten to topple you over. Once the rooms are built on a strong foundation, you will have control over the emotions you experience in those rooms.

Remember, only you have the key to each room, and you will be able to enter and exit them as necessary.

Are you ready?

Let's start digging.

~

N ow that you've constructed the road leading to building your home, you are standing before the glory of your own power to build a home for yourself within yourself.

Why Is a Foundation Essential?

When I was young, there was a picture in my social studies textbook of two families side by side. One picture was of a family that clearly lived a financially rich life. Every person was holding on to a material possession, but you could see misery on their faces. The picture next to it was that of a family sleeping together in one bed, clearly in a small old house, with smiles all over their faces.

It was captioned "Money doesn't buy happiness—a home does."

That image stuck with me. The feeling of home that emanated from the second picture was something I yearned for my whole life.

The question begs itself: What makes a home a *home?*

Is it how big it is? How many rooms it has? How many floors it has? Is it where it's located? Is it how expensive it is?

The obvious answer to all of these questions is no.

If a house is physically made up of a group of rooms, what is it that makes it a home? I would argue that it's the *togetherness* of those rooms or elements—their coming together in one place. Building rooms without a foundation guarantees the collapse of the structure.

Okay, okay. I know you're probably thinking *I know this. You're not telling me anything new.*

I'm not telling you that a foundation of a house is important because I'm assuming that you don't know that. I'm trying to get you to reflect on whether you are together with yourself or not.

Do you have a foundation for your own home? Remember praxis. Do you apply what you know about yourself and your worth to your everyday life?

Imagine a friend came to you and told you that they were struggling with their relationship with their partner because the person is not putting in any effort. Imagine your friend is crying and going on about how they don't feel valued, but, at the same time, they feel stuck because they love this person so much. What would you tell your friend to do? I'm certain that you are an excellent advice-giver when it comes to reminding someone of their worth. You probably would tell your friend to move on from this person, or at the very least confront them. You probably would explain that they deserve better, that they don't have to settle for the hurt someone else is causing them.

I'm also certain you are excellent at talking about what you deserve and what you would never accept less than. You know that if this same person hurt you, you would confront them immediately. And I'm even more certain that you are a master at saying "But my situation is different." You are a master at looking at yourself as an exception to the rules you would apply to everyone else out there.

How much easier would your life be if you took your own advice, right?

So, what's the disconnect here?

The disconnect is caused by the lack of a foundation. My *Why can't I have that?* story blocked my view of the home that I needed to be building within myself. *That*, in my view, existed in others, so I sought it externally. All the elements of the home I needed to build within myself may have been clear to me, but they had no foundation to stand on, because I hadn't done the work that would lead me to the land on which my home would stand. I hadn't broken down the roadblocks in my way. Lacking a foundation for a home within myself led me to attempt to place the elements I had—the knowledge about myself and my worth—inside of someone else. Anyone else. So when they'd reject me, I'd think *How could you not see my worth?!* When the real question needed to be asked in the mirror. Because if I myself saw my worth, I wouldn't base my worthiness on someone else's seeing it.

You see, however you turn it around, a house with no foundation simply cannot be called a house—let alone a home. It's just separate pieces. Your worth cannot be derived merely from your knowledge about worth. It must stand on a foundation that serves two purposes:

1. It puts your own worth inside of you, not inside of someone else.

2. It makes you believe you are worthy of turning your knowledge about your worth into practice.

∽

You can know all there is to know about your worth,
but if you haven't built the right foundation for it,
it will be a flailing element, or room, in the world.
It's not yours. And you have no control over it.
Because you haven't created a base for it to sit on.
You haven't created a spot for it to stay within your control.

∽

You could totally place that room in someone else's home . . . you know, like building a home within someone else. But the risk is that it completely falls apart—that you lose your sense of worthiness—when they walk away.

Boom. It all makes sense now, doesn't it?

So How Do You Build a Strong Foundation?

At this point, I want you to think of the foundation of an actual house. What do you think makes it a good one, a strong one?

A year after I arrived in Canada, my parents decided to build a home for us to move into. I remember driving in the new neighborhood and thinking the area looked dead with so much open space. When we got to our lot, there was a big hole in the ground. Looking at that, I couldn't imagine our future house as a home. I was only seventeen and was still upset we had to move from the house we'd been living in since I'd arrived. My life had been uprooted when I moved from Lebanon, and now they wanted to uproot my home again?

Even though I wanted my own room, my own space, I still couldn't see myself living in this new house. Because my old room, as tiny and as not fully mine as it was, was part of something bigger. It was part of something that felt *together*. I felt safe.

Over the next few months, every time we would visit this house, there would be something new built—a structure, an unpainted skeleton of a home, doors, windows, furniture, and so on. As the home took shape and began to feel more together, I started seeing myself in it.

Even though it took months to start seeing the elements of the home being built, it was worth the wait to have that foundation built to ensure that this home was solid—that it was a safe place to stay. The same applies to the home that you build inside of yourself.

If the purpose of a house's foundation were merely to keep it above ground, building it would be simple and quick. But we all know that the purpose of a foundation is to make sure the house can last forever. It protects it from moisture. It insulates it from extreme temperatures. And it ensures that, should there be any movement in the earth, the house stays intact. In other words, it makes sure that the house and all its elements stay *together*.

So what keeps *you* together?

If the purpose of a foundation is to last, protect, and endure, then the foundation of the home you build within yourself should be made of two things: *self-acceptance* and *self-awareness*.

Why are these the elements of your home's foundation? Because they are about your self.

So just as you'd pour concrete to make a house's foundation, let's pour self-acceptance and self-awareness to make the foundation of your home within yourself. Without these two fundamental elements, you might be able to build the rooms for your home, but it's almost guaranteed that you will place those rooms in someone else's home, because you haven't believed you are worthy of having them within you. And when you have these essential elements for your togetherness inside of someone else, your ability to access them is based on that person's belief in your worthiness of them.

Self-Acceptance

Self-acceptance at its core means knowing yourself as you are, with all your weaknesses and strengths, with all that makes you who you are. Whether you look at those things as flaws or as superpowers is in your own hands.

To accept yourself, you must first know yourself—something that today's fast-paced culture doesn't allow us time to do. Before you can take a breath, a new technology is out, a new app is released, a new trend is emerging. And it becomes overwhelming to keep up with it all. If you don't keep up, you feel left out and isolated. So you'd rather jump on that next new thing instead of truly getting to know yourself and what you want. If you are saying yes to this, then I guarantee you've lost your ability to ask yourself *Is this something that serves me? Or is it just consuming my time?*

We spend money and time on things that give us instant gratification. Some of the lies that we tell ourselves are:

- If I buy this dress, I will feel better.
- If I buy this car, I will feel better.

- If I download this app, I will feel better.
- If I make this much money, I will feel better.
- If (insert your own ridiculous theory), I will feel better.

This *if* on its own indicates your denial of your present, which means that you are not in the state of self-acceptance. To accept yourself, you must have no *if*s. Your current feeling about yourself and your worthiness cannot be dependent on the possibility or probability of something happening. You can have dreams and aspirations but your *I will feel better* should not depend on those dreams and aspirations. You should feel good as you are. You know that material things don't bring you happiness. But there is a difference between what you know and what you do on the basis of what you know.

The current culture would have you believe that accepting yourself as you are means not caring about what people think of you. And don't get me wrong—part of self-acceptance *is* not caring about what the world thinks. But do you see where the flaw in that definition is? It puts the focus on the world—not on you. How could that be self-acceptance? What our culture calls self-acceptance should instead be called indifference to what others think.

Self-acceptance is accepting your *self*. Not caring what the world thinks of this self of yours is a by-product of self-acceptance, not the other way around. As long as your decisions stem from your need, or want, to stand out in the world, you cannot reach self-acceptance. Your decisions must instead stem from your need, and want, to be yourself. To let your inner self shine through. First your light will shine on your own life, and then on the world.

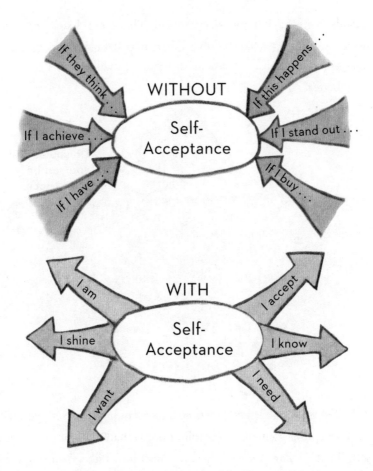

So let me ask you: Do you live your life in a reactive state to the world around you? Or do you live your life because you are fully convinced of your beliefs?

I know most of you reading this are thinking you don't know what your beliefs are . . . perhaps life has become stagnant and you are just going with the flow of what society has dictated life should be like. You go to work (if you work), come home, watch a bit of TV, go on social media, maybe go out and spend some time with

friends, come back home, sleep, repeat. That seems like a pretty ro-
botic life, one in which you've fallen into habit instead of active
decision-making.

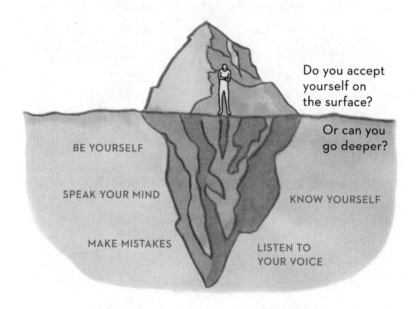

When you don't spend any time understanding yourself, you will
start accepting someone who might not actually be your authentic
self. That's what *shallow* self-acceptance looks like. You might be
accepting a version of yourself that's just a product of your environment. That shallow self involves your ego and what it tells you
about yourself. *Deep* self-acceptance, on the other hand, requires
you to accept who you really are, free of conditioning.

That's deep, isn't it?

You may think you've accepted yourself, but you've only accepted
the image of yourself dictated by those around you, or the person

you were in a specific moment. Let me give you an example. When I graduated from teachers college, I was still very quiet and afraid of raising my voice. When I started teaching at a private school, I constantly found teachers and administrators telling me that I needed to be stricter with my students and not show them my kind side because they would take advantage. Of course, I struggled with that. I didn't want to listen to that advice. I wanted to voice my opinions on how I believe that empathy with students is key to preparing them to learn. But I wasn't used to speaking up. I was conflicted between wanting to listen to these teachers and administrators and wanting to apply my own thoughts and values on education. The mere thought of saying "but I don't believe that's right" terrified me. I had the dangerous disease of trying to please everyone. So instead of confronting my fear of speaking up, I convinced myself that this is how I will always be. I wanted to accept that I was the type of person who just couldn't speak up and say no. That was *shallow* self-acceptance. Because it was in response to my environment.

But, at my core, that is not who I really am. When I was younger, I used to be able to speak my mind if I saw something wrong. I was able to be more unapologetically myself. With every letdown and punishment for doing the right thing, and with every moment of learning to revere men in positions of power, I learned to keep my opinions to myself. That is what led me to be so reserved when I started teaching.

I could have chosen to continue being that person who didn't share her opinions out of fear of being punished for it. Thankfully, my desire to help my students heal overrode my need to stay safe from punishment (or in this case, passive-aggressive treatment). It was through writing that I got to know my true self. I didn't write for many years, and during that time, I didn't allow myself to work through my emotions. Once I started writing again, I started to heal the person who had become afraid of speaking up. And I did not accept the silent me anymore. Through writing, I discovered that the silent me was only a product of my circumstances and my understanding of authority. And, thankfully, I went back to accept the girl who knew she had a voice and that her opinion mattered. That's the me I needed to accept. The whole me. And that, right there, is deep self-acceptance.

So now you might be wondering *How do I know who my authentic self is?* The following tool will assist you with that.

The tools in this room are called anchors because their purpose is to anchor the foundation of your home in one place.

The Clarity room (Chapter Five) will help you immensely with the depth of this question, but for the purposes of building a foundation on which the Clarity room has a place to rest, this is what you need to do.

Anchor #1: Bring Your Authentic Self to Your Awareness

STEP 1: Sit in a place by yourself, in silence.

STEP 2: Listen to what your inner voice tells you. This very likely is not your own, at-home voice. It is likely your ego, which is your sense of self that began to form during your earlier experiences in your life. It is also likely the voices of others and what they've been telling you about yourself. Once you're aware of this, you can imagine pushing those voices away because they really don't define you. You define you.

STEP 3: Tell yourself: *My authentic self is not this voice. My authentic self is listening to this voice. My authentic self transcends time and space. My authentic self is not dependent on the labels or definitions I attach myself to. It is not dependent on my surroundings, people, or things.*

STEP 4: Affirm: *My authentic self is worthy of my own acceptance.* In the process of bringing your authentic self to your awareness, you're automatically incorporating self-awareness, which is a prerequisite of self-acceptance.

∽

Before you accept yourself, you must know yourself.
To know yourself, you must be aware of yourself.

∽

I'd heard those words a billion times. I'd listened to them and thought to myself *Yes, that's exactly what I need to do.* And I would be on this high of *I figured it out!* But that high would fade within a few days, if it lasted a few hours to begin with. You see, the problem was that I was so stuck on understanding myself in my current state that I forgot that this "me" is a product of a history that made me. A product of identities that shaped me to be who I am. A product of expectations of the world around me. A product of certain definitions of right and wrong. Without reflecting on all those elements, I was still ruled by them.

When you come into this world, you are born into an environment that shapes your beliefs for you. And it shapes your idea of who you should be. Most people live their whole lives working toward what that environment taught them is the way to live, without questioning why. The process of understanding the why is what challenges you to take an inventory of your beliefs and allows you to discard the ones that don't serve you, or the ones that don't make sense to you, or simply the ones that you don't believe in.

It's a mistake not to dig deeply into where a belief came from, into our history and journey, into what got us to this moment. Just as you would dig a hole in the ground to start the foundation of your home, you must do the same thing within your own soul, within your own history, to be able to go deep enough to know the authentic you, so you can accept the authentic you.

So the first basic element of your home's foundation that allows you to reach self-acceptance is self-awareness.

Self-Awareness

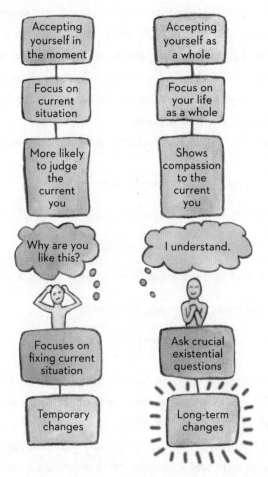

Think of the last time you hung out with people you wanted to fit in with. Perhaps in that context you felt you were in a state of self-acceptance because you felt like you fit into *something*. You fit in *somewhere*. But it's the same as saying *I accept myself* without fully knowing yourself.

This is where, again, the concept of building a home within

yourself proves to be the ultimate goal. Being able to accept yourself in any context, independent of where you are or who you're around, is the true meaning of deep, authentic self-acceptance. Because the focus is not on what's around you, but on what's within you.

So, before you say *I accept myself*, make sure that you are fully aware of the self you're accepting.

Here are some of the *selves* you might be currently accepting:

1. The self your parents raised you to be

2. The self your spouse or partner loves

3. The self you believe you should be

4. The self of the person you're comparing yourself to

5. The self of the person you aspire to be

6. *(Insert the self you're trying to be.)*

When I operated from a place of accepting one of my selves through the eyes of someone else, I was out of touch with my authentic self. Growing up, culture and religion played a big role in how I saw the world. Culture specifically played a role in defining what was right and wrong in terms of being a woman—what was shameful and what was appropriate. Naturally, I believed that any behavior that was not female-appropriate would result in a bad reputation for me and, by association, for my family. So I carried the burden of my reputation and my family's on my shoulders. In my mind, as long as I didn't bring shame on myself or my family, I was on the right track. This became the self I believed I needed to be. And that was shallow self-acceptance at its best. Convincing yourself that the self others believe is "okay" or "good" or "enough" is the self you need to be is shallow self-acceptance.

As I grew older, and after moving to Canada from my relatively sheltered little village at age sixteen, my journey of coming face-to-face with my authentic self began. What did *I* believe being okay, good, and enough meant? I found myself wearing different faces that mirrored the context I was in. For example, during university, I wasn't allowed to go out with my friends if they went anywhere downtown, even if it wasn't a place where alcohol would be served. I understood that my parents believed they were protecting me, but the way it made me feel was isolated and alone. I wanted to go out with my friends, but I couldn't. I wasn't the type to do anything behind my parents' back, so I obeyed while I continued to feel alienated from opportunities for connection outside of a school setting. I understood very well that being in that kind of environment was not a good look for me or my family, so I stayed away. During that time, dating or any kind of relationship with men wasn't even on the table. It wasn't something I allowed myself to think of, because it was just wrong. Fast-forward a few years after I became a teacher and had a lot more autonomy and exposure. This is when I started, bit by bit, to give myself permission to challenge the ways of thinking that had been ingrained in me.

One time, when I was substitute teaching, a male teacher I was working with asked me to stay for a few minutes after the school day was over because he wanted to ask me something. I thought he was going to ask me if I was available to cover for him one day. To my shock, he asked me if I'd go out for drinks. This was the first time a guy had asked me out for drinks. I was twenty-two.

My immediate response was "I can't."

"Why?" he asked me.

"Because I don't drink."

"Okay. What about coffee?"

I still told him that I couldn't: "I don't date."

"Why?"

"It's not how it works in my culture. It wouldn't work anyway, because you're not Muslim."

His answer is one I still ponder to this day. He said, "How is a North American man supposed to learn about your religion if you won't even talk to him?"

I told him he could go to the mosque and learn about it on his own.

He didn't seem convinced. And it most definitely was because I wasn't saying it out of fully believing it, but out of not really knowing how to back my response. I remember feeling so surprised that he asked me when I was wearing a hijab. I thought that kept men away, especially men who were not Muslim.

It wasn't me responding to him. What I had learned was responding to him. Did I personally think that way? I didn't know. I hadn't asked myself that question.

You see, when you don't know *why* you believe something, you don't feel right. Something is off. You are passive in your own life. You lack self-confidence. Other ways this can manifest is that you become defensive, aggressive, or simply withdrawn. Your foundation is unsteady, so you risk your sense of self eroding. And you start projecting an image of yourself that molds into the world around you, rather than bringing your authentic self into the world around you.

Reflecting the world around you keeps
you in conflict with yourself.

Instead, you need to be your authentic self, and
the world around you will change accordingly.

Anchor #2: Reflect on Your Togetherness

1. Do you feel scattered? Lost? Unorganized?

    a. If so, why do you think that is?

2. Are you accepting your shallow self as a way to avoid revealing your deep, authentic self?

3. Have you brought your authentic self into your awareness?

4. Are you projecting your authentic self (reflecting deep self-acceptance) into the world? Or are you projecting one of the aforementioned selves?

    a. If so, which ones?

    b. Are they clashing? (Are you wearing different masks to conceal your authentic self?)

c. How is this manifesting in your life (fear, people-pleasing, agitation, and the like)?

5. Do you know yourself well enough to know what self it is that you are accepting?

In this social media–ruled world, it's hard to define yourself without labels. For the last two or three years, I've been defining myself as an author, poet, healer, and teacher. And before that, when people would ask me who I was, I would rush through saying my name to get to my credentials. My master's degrees. My in-progress doctorate program. I would even pronounce my name as my first teacher in Canada pronounced it, even though she said it wrong: "N-Ah-J-Wa." My name is pronounced *ne-jwa*. And the *j* is very soft. Nevertheless, I'd say *I'm NAHJWA. I am a teacher at X school. I completed my master's degree in curriculum studies in education. I studied multiliteracies and multilingualism. That allowed me to study the factors that affect motivation in second-language acquisition. That allowed me to work with refugees while I pursued my doctorate to study the relevance of curricula and policies to newcomers.* It's a mouthful, huh? But that's how I defined myself.

With labels.

Who was I without those labels? A nobody, I thought.

As long as you are operating from that story, you're not at home with yourself. The following analogy will help you see how the root story, the foundation that you build your home on, will change the outcomes that you live.

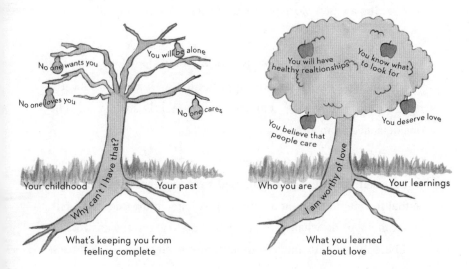

No one wants you

You will be alone

No one loves you

No one cares

Why can't I have that?

Your childhood

Your past

What's keeping you from
feeling complete

You will have
healthy realtionships

You know what
to look for

You believe that
people care

You deserve love

I am worthy of love

Who you are

Your learnings

What you learned
about love

A solid foundation of self-acceptance and self-awareness allows you to see yourself and accept yourself without attaching and using them to define yourself.

Anchor #3: Ask Yourself: Without the Labels, Who Am I?

STEP 1: Write all the ways in which you've been introducing yourself to those around you. At work. In social settings. At school. In other contexts.

STEP 2: Go through those labels one by one and ask yourself: *Who am I without this label? How do I feel about myself if I can't use this label to describe myself?* It's important that you go through them one by one. It's a much more powerful strategy than letting all of them go at once.

STEP 3: Now that you have gone through all the labels, who are you? You don't have to answer this question with words. Answer it from within. Feel it from within. Can you feel the inner you? The one detached from any label?

These steps will lead you to knowing and accepting your authentic core self. I caution you against just reading these steps. It is essential for you to take out a journal, meditate on the questions, talk about them, or do whatever you need to do to get to the answers.

The following formula summarizes the elements of a strong foundation:

Self-awareness ↔ Self-acceptance → A solid foundation

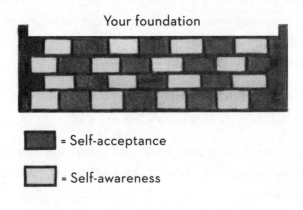

The only permanent residence you are 100 percent guaranteed to have is within your own home.

Don't rush it. Spend time on self-acceptance and self-awareness. Remember that your own home is the best investment you can make. And though the foundation may take a while to build before you can see the full picture of your home, it's worth it.

With all the knowledge I had about self-love, compassion, and kindness toward myself, when it came to the application of it, I was still that eight-year-old girl I told you about . . . the one still asking *Why can't I have that?* and aching for love from an external source . . . the one who was settling for scraps of what people gave her because she genuinely believed that she didn't deserve more. I was still that girl because I wasn't self-aware, and I was at a shallow level of accepting myself. Without healing that little girl and understanding why she learned to believe that scraps of love is all she would ever get, there was no way I was going to understand why I chased after scraps of what people had to give.

Are you in that same place? If you are at a point in your life where you equate self-love with selfishness and you feel guilty for spending time giving yourself love, then you haven't built the foundation for your home. If you are at a point in your life where you rarely feel genuine happiness and are more likely to dip into anxiety or anger over the happiness you want, then you haven't built the foundation for your home. And if you are at a point in your life where doubt consumes you and beats your self-confidence down, then you haven't built the foundation for your home. Most important, if you are at a point in your life where you're dwelling in your pain more than you are in your willingness to heal, then you have definitely not built the foundation for your home.

If there is anything I want you to take away from these pages, it's this: The feeling of home is the feeling of *I'm together with myself.*

This togetherness includes all the elements of your being. In order for you to achieve this togetherness, the foundation of your home is the most important part, because it necessitates your self-acceptance and self-awareness. If there is no foundation, you can have all the elements needed for your home, but the lack of a foundation jeopardizes the control that you have over these elements. Without a foundation, your elements will sit on foundations outside of you: a person, a job, a degree, a title, a stage in life, and so on. Your home is a safe and stable place. In a state of homelessness, chaos and confusion will thrive. You'll look to others for stability, putting yourself at risk of defining yourself and directing the sails of your life according to foundations external to you.

There is no more of that. Now you have a foundation built for your authentic self within you. Your stability is within you. Now it's time to place the elements on top.

Are you ready?

TWO

Self-Love

∾

The goal of this room is to transform self-love from being a cliché buzzword to a mindful practice tailored to you and based on your self-discovery. Just as you would have an individualized meal plan based on your health needs, your self-love practice will reflect your needs as well.

I challenge you to visualize entering this room daily, so when a crisis occurs, you're not tempted to turn to familiar self-hate and other destructive habits. The ultimate form of self-love is for you to be the CEO of the company of *you*.

Are you ready to sit on that throne?

Let's walk in.

∾

Self-love. You might think that you know what self-love is. But now that you've built a strong foundation of self-acceptance and self-awareness, you might want to go into this room, give it a new coat of paint, take out the old dusty furniture, and replace it with real self-love.

First, pull out everything that you call self-love, and let's begin from scratch. Spa day? Shopping spree? A night out?

I'm sure these are some of the first things that come to mind when you think of self-love. And if that's what you need, then that's what self-love looks like. But, I doubt a spa day will heal your childhood trauma and all you've carried from it into your adult life.

You need to enter the Self-Love room every day. This means that self-love is an integral part of your everyday life, not a luxury you treat yourself to every once in a while. Put real work into giving yourself what you need. And after your time in the Self-Love room lets you figure out what you need, you might want to visit another room in your home.

Self-love is a practice. And as I say to my students, practice makes perfect. If you've learned to self-hate, that habit needs to be broken. You can't hate yourself and love yourself at the same time. You can do them both in one day, but you can't do them both at the same time. And once you make self-love a daily practice and taste the sweetness of it, you will want to spend more time in this room. It will transform your life.

Before you can genuinely love yourself, you must believe that you are worthy of love. While constructing the road to your home and building its foundation has brought you the required knowledge and awareness of your worthiness as a whole, the work of self-love now will require a process of rediscovery and unlearning of all that came before in your life.

When you believe you are worthy of love, you will start seeing love around you. You will also start to define yourself by the love you have within you, not the love you receive from external sources. You will start to build boundaries around the love you have within you to protect it as a valuable asset reserved for yourself and those you welcome into your home. Self-love means you do not beg anyone to welcome you into their home or to validate your love by giving it a place to stay.

Let's start with a simple reflection. Picture the person you love the most right now.

What would you do for this person if they came home at the end of the day with a bad headache?

Let me guess. You would do whatever you could to listen and understand and help them out.

What would you do if they were feeling overwhelmed with a task they needed to finish?

You'd help them to your best ability, right?

What would you do if they were feeling insecure or down?

You'd validate them and make them feel safe, right?

So here's another question:

Do you do that for yourself when you're feeling vulnerable or insecure?

Do you give yourself time when you need it? Space when you need it? Love when you need it?

Over the years, as I've encountered people with thousands of different stories, I've realized that most don't know where to start with self-love, because they've never really loved themselves. And, sadly, it's by drawing the comparison of loving someone else that we're awakened to what we've been depriving ourselves of.

I end by saying *Self-love is loving yourself exactly as you'd love the person you love the most. And that love actually feels like love and looks like meeting your own needs.*

Pillar #1: Self-Love Requires Self-Discovery

To be able to dissociate the worthiness of my love from whether others accepted and reciprocated it, I had to take a hard look in the mirror and ask myself why I struggled so much with Noah. The answer was right there in front of me.

When my therapist asked me about the connection I felt with him, I told her: *The first time I met him, I saw sorrow. And I felt this pull to try to help him. And every time he opened up and was vulnerable, I felt a stronger and stronger connection with him. I was familiar with that sorrow. It was comfortable to be in the presence of it. Because I understood it so well.*

I wasn't attracted to Noah. I was attracted to his pain. I wanted to save him. I had this urge to help him heal. One of the first things he told me when we first met was how his last long-term relationship had led him to understand how little he loved himself and that he needed to work on that. Obviously, me being me, I took on the responsibility to rescue him without him even asking for help.

But this was not the first time in my life I felt this deep urge to help someone or save them. One time, while driving to my accountant's office, on the opposite side of the road I could see that an older man had fallen off his bike. He had blood all over his face. I wanted to jump out of my car and help him even though I couldn't get to the other side because of the concrete barrier. And even though I could see that another car had stopped and was trying to help him, I had my hand on my heart for the next few minutes. I cried at the thought of the pain he must've felt. When I arrived at my accountant's office, he quickly pointed out how shaken I seemed. So I told him what had happened.

Since university, I'd been that friend everyone who was struggling would seek out for advice and comfort. Even if they had hurt me in the past. They knew I wouldn't turn them away or judge them. One time, a close friend I'd made during my first year of university completely distanced herself for a few months without explaining to me why. It hurt me, but I didn't say anything about it. Later, we bumped into each other on the bus and we made conversation. She was telling me about a difficult situation she was going through. I listened and offered her understanding. At one point she said, "You're a good friend, you know." I said, "Why are you saying that?" and she said, "Because I really hurt you. And you're still there for me."

She wasn't the first one to point that out. I had the ability to put other people's needs and pains above my own. It's what pushed me to say "It's okay" when someone apologized to me, even though it wasn't okay. All someone had to do to get my attention was display their pain somehow, even just in their body language. And I absorbed it like a sponge. I cry at the thought of someone going through pain. I feel overwhelmed by emotion. Rooms with too many people leave me feeling depleted. And the list goes on.

The first therapist I ever visited a few years ago told me something in passing that I didn't realize the depth of. I was explaining to her how even seeing those who hurt me in pain caused me pain on the inside. She said that it was normal for me to experience that, especially because I'm an empath.

An empath?

"You are highly sensitive and you take on people's emotions as if they're your own," she told me.

Ah. That was a life-changing moment, but one that I didn't allow to change my life at the time. Because instead of asking how I could stop this emotional bleeding, I took on the mentality of *Oh well, that's just how I am. People need to stop pouring their emotions on me.*

But in the Self-Love room, that narrative changes. Putting the responsibility on others to not project their emotions on you is unreasonable. People will do that. You have to develop tools and strategies to balance accepting yourself as an empath while also knowing how to not emotionally bleed at the sight of someone else's pain. Or your own pain. This is an application of self-love: not putting your own emotional well-being at the mercy of the feelings of those around you.

To balance acceptance of yourself as an empath while knowing where to draw the line with your emotional investment in others' emotions, you must first remind yourself that you are worthy of the love you give to others. You are not selfish for giving yourself that same kind of love. Especially if you're an empath, you might feel you're self-absorbed if you take your own love, if you prioritize yourself. As if the love within you was only created to leave

Pouring Out
All of Your Love

Saving Love
for Yourself

you—created to leave you so that once you're emptied out, you have even more reason to want to fill yourself back up, only to have more love to give to others.

IN EACH ROOM, I provide you with strategies to decorate and furnish it in a way that brings its practice to life. In the Self-Love room, these strategies are called gems. I chose gems because they symbolize the valuable and eternal nature of the room.

GEM #1: IMAGINE A PROTECTIVE BUBBLE OF POWER AROUND YOU

This gem will serve as a simple separation between you and your empathy and the emotions of others. Instead of involuntarily being enmeshed in other people's emotions, it serves to remind you that even though you might not have a choice about how you initially react to seeing someone else's pain, it is your choice whether to invest in those emotions. It is your choice how to invest.

Imagine the emotions of others coming at you like arrows. Instead of absorbing them, you stop them at the boundaries of that bubble. This is where you can ask yourself:

1. Is this emotion mine to carry?
2. Am I being asked to carry this emotion?
   a. If yes, do I want to carry this emotion? And do I have the time and energy to do so?
      i. If yes, decide the level of investment that you'll make.
      ii. If no, tell yourself *I have the right to decide not to carry the emotion of this person.*
   b. If no, leave the person's emotion outside your bubble.

This bubble will stop you from emotionally bleeding to the point of depletion. It protects the empathy you have within you.

But isn't a life of service the most noble one you can live? Isn't your ability to be there for others the most noble sacrifice you can make?

I'm here to tell you no. Giving is noble. Loving is noble. But not if you aren't included in that giving and loving.

And if you feel you've always been this way, remember that self-love is a process of self-discovery. So ask yourself, when in your childhood did you develop your way of being? I know for a fact that I learned to give emotionally from my mom. I am convinced she is the kindest person you'll ever meet. She lived her life in the aforementioned way, always giving to the point of depletion and exhaustion, only to give more. She never asked *What about me?* and, for the longest time, I believed that's what being a good-hearted person meant. I see it in my past writings that are currently published! And every time I'd deplete myself in giving and wonder why none of that was being reciprocated, I'd feel like I was being selfish for even wondering that. I felt guilty for actually wanting to receive something. As if wanting to receive anything in return would taint the intention behind why I gave in the first place. And I'd put my ego "in check" and redirect my intention to what it originally was.

But that only soothed my shame. It didn't fix the problem.

I believed that being good meant putting everyone else ahead of me. Or just never putting myself ahead of anyone else. Because the latter would somehow mean I was impure. Selfish. I didn't understand that my upbringing with a mother as *good* as mine caused me to go about self-love the wrong way. With that understanding, I had to do the work to redefine what self-love was.

The question begs itself: *If giving love to others is noble, what is giving love to oneself?* Not selfish, that's for sure.

❧

If loving someone is beautiful, how is loving yourself anything less than beautiful?

If wanting to build a life with someone is beautiful, how is building a life with yourself anything less than beautiful?

If wanting to feel at home with someone is beautiful, how is feeling at home with yourself anything less than beautiful?

❧

Pillar #2: Self-Love Is Embracing Your Authentic Self

You can be the most beautiful gem, but in the hands of someone who doesn't value gems, you will be devalued.

❧

If you define your worthiness of love by the worthiness that others see, you will always find a flaw within yourself, when the simple truth might be you're looking for your worth in the wrong place.

❧

Instead of asking yourself *Why doesn't X love me? What do I need to change about myself so that they can love me? What is it about me that's making them not love me?*, understand that just because someone doesn't love you, it doesn't mean something is wrong with you. It could just mean this person isn't right for you. So quit trying to change yourself in hopes that person will love you. Embrace your authentic self, and the right people will respect you for being authentic with yourself.

Reflecting on my experience with Noah, I thought I was insecure for feeling bothered by his lack of consistency in communication. I thought I was insecure for wanting more than just texting and the odd in-person coffee here and there. I thought I was insecure for wanting to understand where he stood. That's what the Internet told me.

Upon doing deeper research, I came across the psychological theory of attachment styles. According to this theory, there are are four major styles of attachment that people form early in life and carry into adulthood: secure, anxious, avoidant, and anxious-avoidant. A secure person is an at-home person; they're comfortable with connection and don't base their worthiness on external sources of validation. An anxious person is the complete opposite; they're in constant need of validation and come from a place of fear of abandonment. An avoidant person may come across as secure, but they avoid connection out of fear of abandonment. And an anxious-avoidant is a combination of the previous two.

When I read the book *Attached* by Amir Levine and Rachel Heller, I was in for a shock. Upon taking their quiz to understand my attachment style, I found I was mostly secure with a hint of anxiety. For most of my life, until I came to the powerful realization I needed to build a home within myself, I fit into the "anxious" category. Since working on the elements of a home within, I'd learned much, but I still didn't have the foundation. I was still looking at all that knowledge through eyes other than mine. This quiz proved to me that I knew more than what I'd applied in my interactions with Noah and that I knew more than what I gave myself credit for.

So if I was secure with my authentic self, why was I feeling so much anxiety with Noah? It's not because I was desperate for *his* love. It's because I was desperate for love, period. I was in denial of the possibility that we were not on the same page. I wanted this to work. So instead of ending it altogether, I kept questioning myself as a result of his behavior. But it didn't mean that I didn't know my worth. Had I not been bothered by his lack of communication, consistency, and clarity, I probably would still be okay with having an "almost something," a situationship, with him. I would still be holding on.

Since then, I've come up with a simple plan to strengthen relational security.

First, find out your attachment style. Second, work toward being as secure as possible.

I recommend that you find out your attachment style by reading *Attached*, and if you have an insecure attachment style, you should work toward increasing your relationship security. Do this by living as your authentic self, which means you don't change yourself just for the purpose of being welcomed into someone else's home. It means you express your needs even if it means that the other person may turn away as a result. Making someone stay is not your responsibility. And it's definitely not at the expense of your authentic self. Your being your authentic self means you are secure. It means you are not willing to sacrifice your authenticity for someone else's welcome.

You could be secure and still behave anxiously. That's what I did when I held on too long to anyone who was emotionally unavailable. I behaved anxiously out of fear that if I exposed my authentic self, which has a need for clarity, consistency, and communication, I would get pushed away. So I stuck to behaviors based on what I thought I needed (*anyone* welcoming me into their homes) instead of what I actually needed (*me* welcoming myself into my own home within).

It's not that I didn't know what I wanted, it's that I was asking the wrong person.

Pillar #3: Self-Love Is Being Empathetic with Yourself

Moving from being a homeless person to an at-home person requires looking at your conditioning with empathy, not judgment, and working toward changing it. Instead of asking yourself *What is wrong with me?*, ask *What did I go through that taught me to be this way?*

Many of us spend years in therapy trying to understand what is wrong with us, trying to understand current events, as opposed to getting to the root of the problem. And when we can get to the root of the problem, all the current events we go to therapy for will change. Going to the root of the problem entails you tracing back your *Why can't I have that?* story in a way that helps you understand why a certain pattern has persisted in your life. This will allow you to understand yourself instead of judging yourself. It's important to display empathy toward yourself and work toward becoming the person you want to be, as opposed to figuring out what's wrong with you.

GEM #2: WALK IN YOUR OWN SHOES

This strategy will help you display the same level of empathy toward yourself that you would toward anyone you love.

1. Think back to an experience in your life where you find yourself regretting the way you reacted or what you accepted.

2. As an empathetic friend, what would you tell someone who came to you with the exact same story?

3. Say that to your younger self.

One time, I was out with a friend of mine who got out of a marriage of fifteen years. She'd left the marriage three years ago. While talking about relationships, she said, "I accepted so much that I almost believe I deserved to be taken advantage of. I didn't stand up for myself. I didn't leave when I knew I had to leave. I kept making excuses for why I couldn't live without him. I knew that he was abusive, but I hoped that part of him would go away. And look at me now. I wasted so many years of my life living in fear when I could have started my healing so much earlier."

I remember crying during the conversation. I could feel her pain. And I could feel the level of regret and self-blame she was expressing. I told her to remember that what she was looking for was love, not abuse. Safety, not danger. Is that something to be ashamed of? No. I said, "Try to walk in the shoes of the younger you and tell her that. Remind her she was looking for what her younger self, her inner child, didn't get at home. Tell her to let go and promise herself to never search for love in abuse. Tell her how proud you are of her for actually having had the courage to leave."

What would you add?

Now it's your turn to go back to those stories. Now it's your turn to turn to your inner child, your younger self that learned about its worthiness of love long before you became aware of it.

What things do you need to tell your inner child to soothe it? What things should you forgive yourself for?

Pillar #4: Self-Love Is Reflected in the Way You Treat Yourself

The fact that you've already picked this book off the shelf is an indication that you love yourself. Wanting to build a home within yourself to come to at the end of the day, as opposed to begging others for that love, is the ultimate form of self-love.

The late Syrian poet Nizar Qabbani wrote: "The female doesn't want a rich man or a handsome man or even a poet, she wants a man who understands her eyes if she gets sad, and points to his chest and says 'Here is your home country.'"

For years, that's what I wanted. Until I realized that if I don't put my own hand over my chest and tell the person in the mirror *Here is your home country*, no one's chest will ever make me feel home. You may need to say that to yourself, too.

Self-love. The love of oneself. But what does love really mean? What does saying that to yourself actually mean in practice?

We've already discussed that self-love requires self-discovery, that it means being your authentic self, and that it's a practice. But what does *love* on its own mean? In the past, you may have defined love as the love others gave you. You may have learned that love is conditional. You may have learned that love is earned, that it is abusive, that it requires sacrifice. That is now changing. In this Self-Love room, even the people who love you dearly are not allowed to enter. There's another room for them, Compassion.

Love doesn't dismantle your authentic self.

Love doesn't belittle your authentic self.

Love doesn't require you to change your authentic self.

Love is not in words.

Love is in action.

Growing up, I'd always hear a saying in Arabic that's translated as "Love is treatment." In other words, love is about how you treat the one you love. Sure, we want to believe that love is the passionate, butterfly-inducing feeling that we feel toward someone. The depleting urge to be with them. It can feel that way, but it can't *be* that. Love is not self-depleting or tiring. And to love is not about what you feel. It's what you really do with that feeling. For example, when someone says "I love you," does it really mean that they love you if their actions don't show love? Similarly, does it mean that I truly love myself if I just say that I do without actually doing anything about it?

∽

If you say that you love yourself,
what are you doing to show that?

∽

Pillar #5: Being Open to Receiving Love Reflects Self-Love

One day, I visited my brother's house, and as soon as I walked in, my niece Leena, who was three years old, ran to me and hugged me tightly. She always does this, but she was never as glued to me as she was that day. She just sat with me and hugged me the whole time I was there.

I am crying as I write this. Because I am realizing how ungrateful I was for all the world had given me at that point. I was actively choosing not to see all the love around me. As Leena cradled my face in her little hands, it hit me that the only reason I was constantly feeling unworthy of love was that I was blocking my eyes from seeing love from any source other than the places I was seeking love. I was blocking my soul from accepting love that was given to me without working for it. I was blinding myself.

A concrete example would be if you told yourself you would only drink one kind of water. It's a type of water you once drank and felt really nourished by. So, wherever you go, if they don't offer that kind of water, you just don't drink. Even when you're really thirsty. Even though there might be other kinds of water, maybe kinds of water you couldn't imagine, you just don't see them because you're not looking for them. And when you do see them, you tell yourself there's no way they'd make you feel as nourished as the other water did. So you exhaust yourself feeling thirsty and dehydrated just because that one source of nourishment you are looking for is not available. You're probably reading this and thinking . . . that's ridiculous. I would never do that. But you do that with love, don't you?

GEM #3: REFLECT: WHAT LOVE ARE YOU BLINDING YOURSELF TO?

1. Which sources of love do you see? These are the places where you are looking for love.

2. Which sources of love are actually around you? These are the places that are giving you love (like my moment with Leena).

3. What is stopping you from accepting the love that is actually around you? Here, I want you to take the time to write it all out.

Here is an example I'm sure you can relate to on some level. Say you really liked someone who doesn't like you back. Maybe you were in a relationship with this person and maybe not. The focus of your whole being might be on their unwillingness to give you love. If their love is the only source of love you see, you won't see the love that might be coming to you from family, friends, colleagues, and even potential love interests. Because you're not looking for that love. You're not seeing it as a source of love. So, indirectly, you are blinding yourself to the love around you.

You might believe you're not worthy of love, and you've supported that belief with evidence from your past, plus evidence from your current situation. If that's the case, your mind is going to search for every piece of evidence that further proves the story you believe about yourself, or what you make something that happened mean about you. You might see that story referred to as the "ego," which is simply the Latin word for "I." From the moment you wake up to the moment you fall asleep, your ego is looking for proof that reinforces what you believe about yourself. You walk around constantly trying to make everything mean something about you.

When you go to work and say hello to that one colleague you don't even particularly like and they look at you without smiling or saying hello, your ego automatically files that as proof you're not worthy. Whether you are consciously aware of it or not, that's what happens. When you go to the grocery store and the cute guy or girl in front of you looks at you and keeps walking, your brain takes that as proof you're not worthy. Someone not opening the door for you or returning a favor or saying a kind word . . . all of it is registered as proof you're not worthy. Which is what your *Why can't I have that?* story taught you in the first place.

∽

Whatever your brain is looking for, your eyes will see.
If you are looking for the positive, you'll see it. And if
you're looking for the negative, you'll see it.
It's a matter of what you choose to see.

∽

GEM #4: SEE LOVE

As you work on learning self-love, every morning, tell yourself *Today I am going to see proof that I am worthy of love.*

Instead of noticing the people who don't smile at you, you will notice the ones who do. Instead of noticing the people who don't say hello back, you will notice the ones who do. Instead of noticing the lack that you have, you will notice what you do have. And instead of noticing the love that you don't have, you will notice the love that you do have.

(At the beginning of the day)	(At the end of the day)
What I will see today	What I saw today

You might be thinking . . . *but you just said that no one is allowed into this room except me. How can I accept love from others in this room where I'm alone?* Here is what I mean . . . your ability to see, receive, and accept love from others is a healthy sign of you actually loving yourself. Because you genuinely believe that you deserve that love. In other words, it is not the love of others that forms the basis of or nourishes your self-love. It is your ability to see it, accept it, and truly feel it that shows how in self-love you are.

It really is important to clarify that, in the Self-Love room, you're not deriving your self's worthiness of love from any external source. Being able to see your self-worth reflected in the world around you indicates a state of self-worth. So seeing love in several places is a direct result of an inner belief of worthiness of love. Your job is to start training that inner self of yours to start operating from a place of worth instead of from a need for external validation.

∽

*If you set out in the world to see love, you will see it.
And if you set out in the world to see lack of love,
you will see the absence instead.*

∽

Pillar #6: Self-Love Is a Practice, Not a Destination

Practicing self-love is one of the fundamental pillars of this room. Remember how part of self-love is giving yourself what you need? If you need time to heal from something you've gone through, part of self-love is giving yourself permission and time to heal.

A practical application of self-love is building boundaries. I find the term *boundaries* to be overused when we speak and to be severely underused in our actions. Boundaries are not about what you are protecting yourself from. They are about what you are protecting within yourself. Because you value what's within. Building boundaries begins with your knowing and seeing the value of what you are building a boundary around. Imagine them as the protective bubble we talked about earlier. Imagine them as the fence that surrounds your home. And if you've already allowed someone through the gate, imagine your boundary as the door to your house. Boundaries reflect how much you value yourself and what you have within.

Boundaries protect your heart. Your home. And that's why your boundaries aren't based on being in defense mode, but rather being in a self-loving, self-valuing mode. In an *at-home* mode.

We will talk more about boundaries in the Compassion room (Chapter Four).

When you build boundaries, you understand that you get to live on your own terms, by your own rules. You are the leader of your life. You are the manager of your time. You are the CEO of the company of YOU. That means that you heal on your own terms. And sometimes that means that as you heal, you must make decisions for yourself that might potentially hurt others if they perceive them a certain way. But that's their own pain to overcome. For example, as you're trying to heal from a breakup or from a lost friendship or a fallout with someone you were close to at any level, you might need to block their number or remove them from your social media. That might hurt their feelings at first. Your fear of hurting someone else may deter you, especially if you're an empath. Remember, if you're an empath, you'll prioritize protecting someone else's feelings above your own. So on top of trying to heal your own wound, you are worried for the person who was carrying the knife that cut you in the first place. I know that's a very strong way to describe it. And some might be reading this and thinking *Sometimes we hurt our own feelings by interpreting another's actions to mean something they don't actually mean.* Yes, I fully agree with that. I have done it myself many times. However, it doesn't matter whether this person meant to hurt you or not. You're in pain. And keeping yourself in the environment that poisoned you will not take the poison away, whether that poison was intentionally given to you or not. You need to focus on the fact that you are hurting.

And that's where your healing begins. It begins with *Why am I hurting? What can I do about it?*

As you take steps to heal, you might indeed realize that the person who hurt you didn't mean to hurt you. But you won't get to that point right away. You need time and distance in any case. So take it.

Here are a few practical and powerful ways of being the CEO of you.

GEM #5: MEDITATE

I know meditating might seem like an overused suggestion. But it is so powerful. I remember always hearing this and thinking *I don't need to meditate. I am always calm with the people around me. What I need is an outlet for my pent-up anger. I need something more like axe throwing.*

As I write this, I am laughing at myself. But at the same time, I understand my past self. I always thought that meditation was somehow supposed to relieve me. To help me breathe. And now I know that to be true, but I also understand what that relief really means. The reason meditation relieves you is that it allows you to understand who you are, now, in the moment. I always thought I was doing it wrong because, as soon as I was quiet for one minute, my brain would go crazy, and I would just say *This isn't working.* When, in reality, I didn't know what the purpose of meditation was and how relief was achieved.

I also didn't know that this was a process. I expected the result to be immediate. And it makes sense that if what I was looking to relieve was my anger or resentment or blaming of myself or others, there was no way that sitting in silence while thinking all those thoughts and feeling all the feelings those thoughts led to was going to give me any relief. It was only going to intensify them. It's akin to giving a fire more oxygen; the fire will only get bigger. If my true purpose during that silence is to understand myself—deeply understand who I am, not the feelings at the surface—then those feelings will have less and less power, and I can be the one with power over my life.

So how do I meditate? I just sit in silence. Start with five minutes. Keep all your electronics and any other distractions away. And just listen to yourself. Listen to what your mind is telling you. You might have an overflow of negative thoughts when you start, which is great! Because now you are actually becoming aware of what your mind is telling you. Only when you become aware will you be able to accept the thought and what it's causing you to feel—and then make a choice about it. For example, you've just started meditating, and the first thought that comes to your mind is of a person who mistreated you, and you get this sense of urgency and panic to do something about it. You have two choices here. Either you follow this thought and feeling and end up at *I'm never going to find love* or *I'm not worthy of love.* Or you can say to this thought and feeling *I see you. I accept that I am thinking and feeling you. And I understand that you are coming from my mind. But you are not who I am. You are not welcome as a permanent resident in my home. You are here because my mind is thinking you, because my heart is feeling you, but you are not me. And I choose not to follow you.* You see, how beautiful does that sound? The act of accepting a thought and the feeling that it leads to, or vice versa, takes away from its power. It takes away from the state it's trying to put you in or lead you to. Now you become the leader, the decider, the chooser of where you go.

This is not a state you attain and then you're there forever. It bothers me when people ask "How do you stay positive all the time?" I'm not positive all the time. Negative thoughts visit me. Negative feelings visit me. And instead of pretending they're not there or ignoring them, I actually listen to them and try to understand where they're coming from, whether I choose to continue to think or feel them (which I rarely do), and then I let them go. The following poem is one I'll be sharing with you as a reminder throughout the rooms:

When pain knocks on your door,
welcome it.
Let it in.
Sit with it.
Have tea with it.
Understand it.
Then let it leave.

Because there's another feeling waiting at the door waiting to be felt by you. There's another thought waiting to be thought by you. And the real power with this is that you are the one who opens the door and you are the one who walks your guest back outside.

As I will explore in the Surrender room (Chapter Six), pain comes in different forms. It could come as anger, resentment, guilt, betrayal, letdown, and so on. The harder it knocks (which means you are ignoring it), the louder it becomes. Eventually, it's so loud you can't ignore it, or you get used to a life with that much noise in the background without knowing how much more serene your life would be without it. So the mere act of welcoming it in gives you the power to decide what to do with it. Yes, there are some feelings that will come in sheep's clothing, disguised as something they're not.

For example, what you might think is guilt could really be shame. Guilt means you believe you *did* something wrong, whereas shame means you believe that *you* are wrong. And once you welcome a feeling in, you might realize you are in for a much bigger challenge than you thought you were in for. However . . . the answer is never to ignore what you're feeling or thinking. That has no potential of solving it. It only exacerbates it.

So, back to meditation. Just listen. And be the manager of where your thoughts go. Don't be ruled by where they take you or who they make you believe you are. That is all part of self-love.

As a result of this meditation, you might find that you need to visit another room in your home. Knowing what you need to do for yourself next is also part of self-love.

GEM #6: SET A SELF-LOVE INTENTION FOR THE DAY

Five minutes is 0.3 percent of the time you have in one day. But this 0.3 percent can transform your life. Literally tell yourself *I am going to spend five minutes in self-love mode*. You can begin by reading the following affirmations:

1. I am the only person in charge of loving myself.

2. I will see evidence of love throughout my day.

3. I am my number one priority. I deserve my own love.

4. Loving myself means being at home with myself.

5. My whole power is inside of me.

6. Today I will answer my own call for love.

7. I understand that I might have moments of falling back into old habits rooted in self-hate or unworthiness, but I promise myself to practice self-love any moment I become aware of my own negative self-talk.

Here is a powerful way to bring awareness to your self-talk: **Switch to self-love mode.** Imagine flipping the switch in a room to turn the light on. You're doing the same thing here. Ask yourself *Is the feeling I'm feeling or the thought I'm thinking coming from a place of self-love?* This is a simple way to snap yourself out of speaking to yourself from a place of self-sabotage or belittling. I love this tool because it allows you to be aware of how you're feeling and thinking while simultaneously giving you the power to change it. To flip the switch on means that you've caught yourself speaking to yourself without love and now you're speaking to yourself the way you'd speak to someone you love.

For much of our time, especially in this age of social media, we spend countless hours aimlessly scrolling through our phones, hoping for something to happen—perhaps a notification to pop up, or a piece of information to bring us some form of relief. It's all a distraction from our present. It takes us away from the power of the present moment with the hope that something external will make us feel better about ourselves. We give away our power over what we do with our time, because we would rather invest time in the uncertain than in the certain. The uncertain is the possibility of something external to us making us feel better. The certain is our current situation. We are constantly looking for an escape.

Stop waiting for something to happen. Stop waiting for someone to save you. Stop waiting for answers. Stop waiting for love. Stop waiting for the right moment, for the right situation. Stop waiting for relief. Stop waiting for clarity.

To bring this to a practical level, how many times do you find yourself scrolling through your phone aimlessly, waiting for something to happen? Or spending every moment you're not working, studying, or doing whatever it is that you do, in texting, calling others, watching a show, and so forth? And it all feels like the feeling you get when you're continuously eating but not getting nourished. You're ingesting so much that it overwhelms you, but you still feel empty. This happens when you're subconsciously waiting for something to happen that will take you out of the situation you're in, whatever that situation is. It's like you are waiting for someone to roll out the red carpet to their home for you. Or waiting for that one event or change that will transform your life completely, that will bring you happiness.

All that waiting is an escape. An escape from your reality. A denial of it. And indirectly a judgment of it.

No man can save you. No woman can save you. No one can save you. No amount of money, status, fame, or wealth can save you. Changing your mindset about being saved is what will save you. If you were to build a home for yourself within yourself, you would be giving yourself the safety you need, the love you need, so when you look at others, you don't feel in need of them welcoming you into their homes. And at the same time, you don't perceive your own home, your own self, at such a low value that you're just willing to place it all in someone else with the hopes that they will be your foundation. If your home felt so safe to you and so welcoming of you, why would you be constantly reaching out to someone else or something else to give you those feelings?

GEM #7: STOP WAITING

So what do you do in this case? How do you stop waiting?

1. RECOGNIZE. Be aware of when you are waiting. It feels like a state of restlessness. Or a state of complete numbness. A sad kind of numbness or a completely detached from reality kind of numbness. It's easier to recognize this state of waiting when you look at your day-to-day life over time and look for patterns in how you spend your time.

2. UNDERSTAND. Understand what you are waiting for.

3. REFLECT. Are you giving up your own power? If so, what/ who are you giving your power to?

4. RECLAIM. Take back your power from the "what if" and give it to the "what is."

This is the most important step. You are taking back the power you've surrendered to the uncertainties and unknowns, and you're giving it to what's certain and what's known. And what is certain? That you are the owner of your power. You are the leader of your own life. You are the builder of your own home. You are the decider of your happiness. You are the CEO of you.

Pillar #7: Self-Love Is Realizing Your Own Power

Your power is inside of you. The love you have within you is your power, not what you get in return for it. Not whether someone deems it worthy of being taken.

With Noah, I depleted myself to give love to someone who wasn't ready to take that love. And his inability to take it made me lose sight of the fact that I am not defined by the love that others accept from me, but by the love I have within me.

If you were to spend the day cooking a meal for your partner to show them your gratitude and they came home and didn't even try it, how would you feel? Probably that that meal and the time put into it was not valuable, right? Well, let's see if that's true. Does someone's not eating it take away its nutritional value or how delicious it is? No. But your intention and end goal was to receive validation from your partner, to feel what you had to give was received by someone you care about. Because somehow that would mean there is value to what you had to offer, which means that *you* have value.

What if your intention of cooking the meal was simply to cook the meal to your best ability? Would you feel that it's worthless simply because someone, whoever that person is, didn't eat it? Probably not.

You see, once we stop evaluating the worth of our love by who receives it, or whether it's received at all, or the type of reaction we get as a result of giving it, that's when we can see the worth of our love on our own. In our own home. Not through the lens that someone else, in their own home, is judging it with. If you made a pie and took it to your neighbor's home and they said to you "Thank you, but we actually don't eat dessert," would you sit at their doorstep waiting for them to change their mind and eat it in order for you to feel like the pie had value? The only time you'd actually linger in front of that neighbor's door is when you have no home to return to. But when you do have your own home, you'll be able to go back to it and eat the pie yourself. Or serve it to someone else who actually likes pie.

Don't equate your worth with whether the pie is eaten or who eats it. That's exactly what we do when someone *rejects* us. I used to love the word *rejection*. I've written hundreds of poems on it. But now it doesn't even exist in my dictionary. Rejection does not exist. The only rejection that exists is the rejection of the self, period. Being in a state of anything but *at home* is rejection. Because being at home entails self-acceptance and self-awareness, remember? If you truly and genuinely accept yourself, then that includes the love within you. And if you accept that love, then you don't define its value by who takes it or what they give you in return for it. And you wouldn't feel so desperate to give it just to feel it has value. Doing that means you're defining your value only by what you do, not by who you are.

∾

Before you give love to someone in any form,
ask yourself, Is my intention to truly love this person?
Or is it to receive validation that my love is worth it?

∾

Have you ever experienced a vulnerability tantrum? I define this as *wanting so badly to be vulnerable but being so afraid of it that you end up swinging between the euphoria of the thought of being vulnerable and the fear of the consequences of it.* I used to experience these tantrums often. Why did I want to be vulnerable? Because I wanted to feel a stronger connection to people, to life, to here, to now. And what was I afraid of? I was afraid that rejection of that vulnerability would make me feel I'd betrayed myself.

One time, after I'd ended my communication with Noah (before the final end that I told you about at the beginning of the book), he basically begged me to hear him out. He said he was going to open up about his past and tell me why he was so guarded. I listened to him, but I didn't know what his intention in telling me all of this was. He still didn't express what he wanted from me. In retrospect, he just didn't want me to be the one to end communication with him. This was all about power.

After he opened up, I was very careful with our communication. The empath in me felt in my gut that something was off. So I experienced this push and pull between being vulnerable and not vulnerable. What stopped me from being vulnerable with him wasn't that I didn't trust him, it was that I associated being vulnerable with giving up my power. I was afraid that if he shut me out again after my being vulnerable, it would have been my fault for being vulnerable in the first place. I expressed my fear to him and he reassured me that this time, it would be different.

After a few days on end of texting nonstop, which, I thought, had to somehow turn into an actual meeting, he stopped texting me. I waited it out.

The first day was okay.

The second day was okay.

The third day, I started to feel a bit of anxiety.

The fourth day, it got worse.

And on the fifth day, it got even more worse.

I was doubting myself. I was feeling so powerless. Why was I feeling so powerless? Why was I waiting for a text message? Because I equated my vulnerability with giving up my power. Because I felt I'd betrayed myself by overlooking what my gut was telling me by believing him when he said that this time would be different.

But the truth is, my ability to believe him and give him another chance at being clear and consistent with his communication showed my empathy. My power. His inability to honor the promise he made did not take away my power. My vulnerability did not make me powerless. My vulnerability IS part of MY power.

~

If someone chooses to take advantage of your vulnerability and not honor the promise that they made to keep a safe space for your vulnerability, that's on them. It's not on you. And it doesn't mean you are powerless. Your power is like a well that never runs out of water. People may drink from it. People may take way too much at a time. But you are the source of that power.

~

Pillar #8: Self-Love Means You Start Answering Your Own Call for Love

When was the last time you were upset with yourself for not meeting your own needs? Not in a self-deprecating kind of way where you ask yourself *What is wrong with me?* I mean upset for not taking responsibility and accountability for meeting your own needs. Perhaps it looked like constantly questioning why this person or that person was not being considerate of your feelings or why they don't care about you.

Next time you find yourself waiting for validation from someone, whether it's in the form of a text message, a phone call, or any form of communication, ask yourself *What is that validation really going to do? What is it going to tell me about myself? What is it going to RE-ALLY change for me?*

Is it going to tell me that I am worthy? Is it going to tell me that I am okay? Is it going to tell me that it was okay for me to vulnerable? Do I really need that validation from an external source?

I found myself in this place over and over again. I recall one day when, in a moment of waiting for a text message from Noah, I heard this voice in my mind that said *How could you betray yourself? How could you not answer your own message? How could you not give yourself a call?*

He is not betraying you. You are betraying you.

And that's how you strip yourself of your own ability to build a home within yourself. When you don't see the value or the beauty of your own home, collectively made by the elements in it, why would you ever want to build it? Why would you ever want to live in it?

I put self-love early in the book because it's one of the most important and most incorrectly defined and understood elements of our oneness with ourselves. You can tell yourself all you want that self-love means you don't allow people to treat you in a way that makes you feel disrespected or unworthy. But that's not what self-love is. You see, when the focus is on the other, the power is with the other. Loving yourself is about *your* self. Remember, the state of being at home with yourself means that wherever you go and whoever you're surrounded by, you are at home. Because you are in control of yourself. Because you are in an authentic state of self-acceptance and self-validation. Your being, your *at-homeness* is not affected by the acceptance or rejection of the outer world, whether it be a guy or a girl, a job, family, a social circle, or whatever. As long as your definition of self-love involves others, you are not in a state of self-love. You are in a state of feeding your ego—the false story you tell yourself about yourself.

GEM #8: ANSWER YOUR OWN CALL

I came up with this tool and placed it in the Self-Love room as a reminder to stop expecting others to do or say something so you can feel better about yourself. It is a reminder to stop waiting for any symbol of someone else showing up for you. Whether it's a phone call, a text, an email, a gesture of love. Whatever it is. Stop hanging your okayness and enoughness on someone answering your call. Stop expecting someone to answer your call before you answer your own. Every time you ask yourself *Why is this person not valuing me?* turn the question to yourself and ask *Why am I betraying myself, my home, by giving someone else so much power over my own worth, over my own feeling of home? What do I need to give myself right now?* And give it to yourself.

So, we've approached the end of this chapter. And as we do, I hope you're approaching the end of your fight to be loved by others. There is a beautiful irony in pain and endings. Remember earlier, in the Introduction, when I said that at the end of my conversation with Noah *This was the end of the fight?* In hindsight, this was the end of the fight I had been fighting my whole life . . . the fight to beg someone to love me. I finally heard what all those painful endings were trying to tell me: *I'm begging you to love me.* The *I* was my authentic self. And the *you* was the twenty-nine-year-old me who was still asking *Why can't I have that?*

Listen to yourself. It's telling you *I'm begging you to love me.*
Will you answer the call?
This Self-Love Contract will help.

GEM #9: SIGN YOUR SELF-LOVE CONTRACT

Read this contract carefully, and sign it. Come back to it as often as
you need to.

> I am the source of my love. I am the one in charge of fulfilling
> my own needs and wants. I am the one in charge of healing what
> my childhood taught me about myself and my worthiness of
> love. It is my responsibility to not shrink or break myself into
> pieces so that others can welcome me into their homes. It is
> my responsibility to build a home within myself and welcome
> myself as I am. At once whole, healing, and a work in progress.
>
> I may not feel whole right now, but I fully understand that
> my authentic self deserves to be loved. And the first one to love
> me is me. When I do that, no one can make me feel less worthy
> by withholding love. If I am not welcomed into other people's
> homes, I will not make that mean anything about me. I will not
> take it personally. Because I understand that there is no way for
> me to feel homeless as long as I have a home within myself for
> myself.
>
> I may not have completed building my own home yet, but
> I will not beg anyone to welcome me into their home in the
> meantime. My own home is the one worthy of all my love and
> energy. And until that home is complete, I will not use others
> to make me feel home. All that I am willing to give someone
> just so they can love me in return I will direct toward building

my own home. I will do the work it takes to go back to the beginning of my pain, to my *Why can't I have that?* story and heal all the lies it told me about myself.

I love myself.

Sign here:

_____

THREE

Forgiveness

In this room, you will learn how to cut the chains of pain that are holding you down. You will learn that forgiveness is not at all about the person who hurt you. Forgiveness is about you. Forgiveness is about letting go.

Forgiving yourself allows you to let go of the person you thought you needed to be. Forgiving others allows you to accept what happened and let go of needing to change it.

You will enter this room anytime you feel you are struggling with letting go of how someone has pained you. You might find yourself entering this room daily or every once in a while. And that's okay. Forgiveness takes time and reflection. Be patient with yourself.

Are you ready to start letting go?

Let's begin.

B efore you walk into this room, ask yourself *What does forgiving someone mean?*

Whatever your answer is, I want you to leave it outside the door for a bit and try to answer it again after you read this chapter.

As you enter the Forgiveness room, you are aiming to let go of the pain. You are aiming to accept, not reverse, what happened. You are aiming to rise above the pain by walking through it.

You enter the Forgiveness room for your own sake, not for anyone else. No one else is allowed in this room but you. Do not seek a cure from the person who caused you pain. Do not wait for their apology to give yourself permission to feel the pain. If you do, you will only cause yourself more pain. And as long as you do that, you are giving them more power over your own healing. And that's something you are choosing to do. This sounds like tough love, doesn't it? I am giving it to you because you need it. And because you deserve better than to believe you don't have as much power as you actually do. Remember one of the integral rules of the Self-Love room: *Your power is inside of you.*

So if being in the Forgiveness room hurts too much because you are bringing the person who hurt you in with you, take a short trip back to the Self-Love room and remember that taking ownership over your healing is key. Remind yourself to answer your own call. Remind yourself that you are your number one priority. Remind yourself that what you look for is what you will see.

The one in charge of letting go of the pain inflicted on you is you. Not anyone else. I guarantee that even if the person who hurt you came back to you right now and admitted what they did and said they regret it, it will not take away the pain. It might for a little bit. But that's just a patch, a Band-Aid.

Someone can't be the pain and the cure at the same time. They can be the instigator of the pain, but they cannot be the healer of it. You have to be. And chances are, whatever pain they activated within you had to be activated at some point in your life. I'm not asking you to thank them for it or to say you are grateful they caused you the pain. Even extending them gratitude for pain would give them power.

You are not the reason
an arrow was aimed at you.
You are not the reason
an arrow brought you to your knees.
But you
are the only reason
that you chose to get up
off your knees
with blood on your hands
and tears in your eyes.
It is the resilience in your spine,
in your veins,
that takes the credit,
not the misery that gushed
from their hearts
to release an arrow at you.

Understand that it is never okay for someone to hurt you. Don't try to justify it. Aim to make sense of yourself and why you reacted the way that you did.

When you forgive them, you are saying *What you did to me happened. It was not okay. Putting this behind me doesn't mean that I am minimizing it. It means that it no longer has power over me.*

So before you enter this room, ask yourself:

1. What/who do I need to forgive?

2. Am I ready to forgive?

3. Have I felt the pain yet?

4. Have I understood what it's trying to teach me? (If not, make a visit to the Surrender room.)

The Forgiveness room will not serve as a magical vending machine that provides an instant outlet for your pain once and for all. Some pain requires years to fully forgive. Forgiveness is a practice in letting go.

When I started writing this chapter, I had no idea what kind of a ride I was in for. After countless hours of working on all the pillars I had in mind for forgiveness, I knew something was missing. The more I wrote, the more I felt I needed to write. I found myself one day at a random coffee shop writing at the top of my page *Who do I forgive?*

Who do I forgive?

How far back do I have to go?

I could feel discomfort inching its way through my body to my eyes. To my fingers. And I just sat back and closed my eyes. I didn't care who was looking at me. I didn't care what they were thinking. I could feel the sun hitting my face. And it all started flashing in front of me.

Who do I forgive?

How far back do I have to go?

Where do I even begin?

Pillar #1: Having Someone or Something to Forgive Is Not Shameful

It's not up to you what pain is thrown your way or how long it takes to heal. What's up to you is what you choose to do with that pain once it enters you. If you choose to resist it just because you think you, at this stage in your life, shouldn't be feeling this pain, then it will stay there. I often use the analogy of someone knocking on your door. If you continue to ignore the knock, it will only get louder and more annoying with time. Even as you ignore the knock, you will have to adapt your behavior to when it begins, how loud it is, and when it stops. In other words, it's controlling you. You're fooling yourself if you think not allowing it in is going to make it go away.

When pain knocks on your door:

> *Let it in.*
> *If you don't, it will knock*
> *harder and harder.*
> *Its voice will become*
> *louder and louder.*
> *So let it in.*
> *Spend some time with it.*
> *Understand it.*
> *Then walk it to the door*
> *and tell it to leave*

because it's time for you to welcome
happiness.

It's the same story if you deny that someone has hurt you badly enough to warrant forgiveness. Maybe because you don't think that the pain is severe enough, maybe because you think someone as "strong" as you should be able to withstand the pain.

It is not strength
to look down on a pain
that is towering over you.

Walk with me a few years back. I'm sitting in front of a superior of mine at work. I'm in a state I can only describe as complete de-realization. Everything around me is blurry. The expression on her face is the exact opposite of the one she showed me the day we first met, the day that I came forward. On that day, she thanked me for my bravery, hugged me, and said that I was going to be okay, that she was going to protect me from that man. Now, she looked at me with an *I just need this to be over* look, without a hint of emotion, and said "You *need* to put this behind you." I'm looking down at my lap and can feel my tears soak through my pants onto my legs.

My tears at this point are waterfalls. Quiet waterfalls.

How did I go from being the perfect girl, the perfect daughter, the perfect student, the perfect teacher, the girl whose principal asked her to stand up in front of the rest of the school and said of her "I want you all to be like her." How could I go from being that girl to this one? To being indirectly called a liar?

Wasn't this system supposed to believe me? Wasn't it supposed to protect me? As a young woman with a vast intersectionality of identities that further made me vulnerable, wasn't this due process supposed to be fair?

I can't tell you what part of the pain was the worst in that moment, but I can tell you that it wasn't just one pain. It wasn't that the results went against me. Or that people I looked up to had let me down or judged me. It wasn't that I had to return to a workplace where the person who caused me all this pain was still in power. It wasn't the denial of the story. It wasn't all the inconsistencies and questions no one answered for me. It wasn't those who lied about me. It wasn't the vision of my doomed career. It was all of that. And, worst of all, it was that when I walked out that door, I didn't know where to go, or who to go to or what to do. It was that when I walked out that door, I didn't know who I was. At that point, my family didn't know. None of my friends knew. I was the strong one. I was the one who wasn't supposed to have taken this kind of fall in the first place.

I had relied on a system outside of me to take my shame away. In a way, I'd built a home for myself in that system. And maybe if the results were in my favor, I would have been able to deconstruct that shame over time with the validation of those whose voices carried so much power. But the sad truth is that no finding by any system could go back to the root of the shame and completely get rid of it.

I had to do that.

Throughout my years here in North America, I'd remember all the direct and indirect messages I'd get that women are given more rights and are more respected here than where I'd grown up. Even though that may be true in many contexts, based on my experiences with the system, that was not my lived experience, nor is it that of most women who come forward. The oppression of women takes on different forms around the world and is often hidden behind cloaks of policies and slogans that serve to protect deeply ingrained misogynistic hierarchies of power.

Pillar #2: Forgiving Someone Doesn't Happen Under Their Roof— It Happens Under Yours

Let's go back to the coffee shop. As I leaned my head back against the window that day, I judged myself for thinking that I had so much to forgive. *Was I being ungrateful for everything I had by focusing on what needed to be forgiven? Did my inability to let go mean that something was wrong with me?* So I changed the thought . . . I told myself that having something to forgive does not make you less than others. It doesn't mean you are weak. Just because you can't let it go doesn't mean something is wrong with you.

I ask you: Have you stopped opening up to others about how much you're struggling with letting go of a person, event, or pain? Maybe you're worried you've become a broken record. A burden. You're sick of your own self. And so you go back to hiding your pain, just as you did before you finally opened up about it.

Was it about time for me to just let go of my past? I'd already had the courage to break so many boundaries by then. Breaking those boundaries was like facing my own death. In a beautiful way, I was facing the death of the woman I'd been taught to be. The woman I'd been told to be. The woman I'd been convinced that, once I became her, I'd be happy.

I was facing the death of that woman just by considering what I really wanted to do. No, no. I was facing the death of that woman just by thinking of getting myself to think of what I really wanted to do.

Truth be told, I had no idea what I wanted. I had no idea who I was. I had absolutely no idea.

I'd put all my energy into fulfilling expectations. I took pride in working every waking moment of every day. In not sleeping because I had so much on my mind that needed to be done the next day. That made me a hard worker. And that right there was an emblem of honor.

I have to preface this next part by saying I understand that many who belong to the Muslim faith and the Arab culture might read this and think that I'm painting a flawed picture of both the faith and the culture. That is not my intention. Our lived experiences always differ, but it serves no purpose to hide some stories or ignore their existence just for the collective image of a faith or culture. So the following is not an attempt to say that everyone who comes from my faith, culture, or background has had the same experience. My intention is to tell *my* story, how I experienced it.

I started attending an Islamic school when I was in seventh grade. At recess and lunch, girls and boys were separated. The boys had basketball nets on their playground, but we didn't. Their playground was twice as big as ours. The playgrounds were on either side of the school, and there was a big walking path between the two with a high metal gate that was opened only at the end of the day, when buses came to take us all home. While boys had gym class, we had art class. One time in art class, another student was talking about how she couldn't imagine marrying a man without loving him. Our teacher got very upset and said "Love is not what you think it is. You marry a man first and then you learn to love him."

I never gave myself the right to think about boys. Because boys could be thought of only when marriage was part of the conversation. That's what I learned as part of our curriculum. Was it that I never gave myself the right to think about boys, or was it that I wasn't given that right? I don't really know. All I know is that talking to boys was wrong. I didn't know how to talk to boys.

We understood very early on in school that men had privilege over women. They were the protectors. They could do a lot more than we could do because . . . they simply were men. For example, they were allowed, even encouraged, to wear cologne, while we were taught that wearing perfume is the equivalent of having sex with a man you're not married to—one of the biggest sins you could commit. Because I trusted my teachers, mostly men, I trusted that those teachings were based on the Quranic text. Only in my later years did I come to learn that most of those teachings were man-made and had no root in Islam.

Almost every girl in our class had a crush on a boy and thought she was in love. But dating or talking about feelings among girls and boys was forbidden. Those kinds of conversations were for marriage and, naturally, getting married was the dream. It was the end goal. For most of the girls. It wasn't my dream.

My dream was *that*. Love. Home. Belonging.

I always walked around knowing, feeling, that something was missing. I always felt malnourished.

Until one day.

When I was fourteen, one of my teachers at that Islamic school started making me feel special. He'd call our house late at night, introduce himself to my dad as my teacher, and say he wanted to explain some concepts I needed help with. He would then proceed to talk to me about life. I was fourteen. Fourteen. He told me he'd never met someone so mature. So kind. So understanding. He told me I reminded him of how good of a person he could be. I got attached to the attention he gave me pretty quickly. One day, my friend Mariam invited me over to her house after school. This was a rare occurrence because she lived in another village, so this happened only when I could ensure a ride home. I had mentioned that plan to him. And he actually went to my friend's house and sat with us outside. We were fifteen at this point, so I guess that's why no one suspected anything. I don't know what his plan was, but I felt so good and so ashamed at the same time. In a way, when I couldn't find *that*, I took whatever felt like it. It ended when I visited my family in Canada that summer; soon after, he married a sixteen-year-old.

This wouldn't be the last time a considerably older man who I looked up to would show me the kind of attention that made me feel special. The last time this happened was a few years after I arrived in Canada. That story marked the end of my need to please men, especially men in positions of power. Because a professional setting and a power differential were involved, I did file a harassment complaint and was met with a typical denial of what had happened. That's the moment in a superior's office I described earlier.

Do you know what the beauty in the denial was? It felt like someone took a calendar and blocked out years of my life from it. Their attempt to erase the pain that had been a permanent resident inside of me felt like an erasure of my own self. But that was the beginning of the detonation of one powerful bomb: my voice. What came after that moment taught me what forgiveness was. It taught me that when you place the foundation of your home—your self-acceptance—under the roof of the person who gave you pain, you'll never see yourself as worthy of your own home.

I did not learn the real meaning of forgiveness until I forgave that man. Under my own roof. In my own home. With my voice. My truth.

And it all started with understanding my story through my eyes.

Pillar #3: Forgiving Yourself Strengthens You

> *My dear self,*
> *forgive me for all the times I said*
> *it's okay*
> *when I should have said*
> *it's not okay*
> *or*
> *I forgive you.*

I judged myself for the way I so innocently fell for the attention of someone I admired. In a way, falling for the attention was a reflection of how little I thought of myself. For the longest time, I kept trying to make things go back to "normal" with him. And it took me a long time to understand that it never *was* normal. He was someone I looked up to. The relationship should never have crossed that line. And I needed to constantly remind myself that I was not the one who crossed that line first.

I judged myself for having a hard time letting go of the ever-so-toxic attachment I had to him. Was it him? Or was it the attention?

Was it the attention? Or the attention of a man who had power and status in the community around me? Was it my need to please someone with so much power? Was it my need to feel I had value as a teacher, as a human, as a *woman*?

Forgiving myself meant that I understood myself. It meant that I looked at my younger self, who'd never learned that saying no was okay. It meant going back to my younger self and telling her:

> *Forgive me for blaming you*
> *for what you didn't know.*
> *Forgive me for blaming you*
> *for what they chose to do.*

In the process of forgiving myself, I reflected on the conditioning of my younger self. That was an essential part of my healing. Making sense of the pain and the trauma was not enough. I had to make sense of myself. I did not heal from my trauma merely by making sense of the events that led to it. I had to take a hard look at my life as a whole and the cultural and religious conditioning I grew up with. I saw that my conditioning was benign and malignant at the same time—benign in how long it took for me to realize that change needed to happen and malignant in how destructive it was to my whole being. Making sense of it all led me to understanding myself.

Making sense of why you reacted the way you did to a painful event will increase your self-awareness and knowledge of yourself. It will help you be more empathetic with yourself. And that eases self-forgiveness.

Do not focus your healing on making sense of why someone would want to cause you pain. You will never know their true intentions or whether they actually intended to hurt you or not. It's better to aim to accept instead of to decode, dissect, or justify what happened. Getting stuck on trying to make sense of it is a form of resistance to feeling it or an escape from it. And all that is a distraction from doing the real work. From going back to the root and extracting the pain from the source.

I did not heal from my trauma by understanding what happened at a logical, conscious level. My trauma still shows up in my life. My healing means that I am aware of it. Making sense of trauma does not mean you won't be triggered to go back to it. Trauma feels like an invisible organ inside of me separate from my heart that, in certain situations, and simultaneously with my heart, beats pain into my veins. Part of self-forgiveness and healing is accepting the pain when it comes and not judging myself.

Through therapy and extensive journaling, I came to understand my trauma. To understand my triggers. And I understood that they would show up every once in a while. I could not have this home within me right now without that acceptance.

∼

You have to welcome the pain when you feel it,
not just know where it came from.

∼

"But, Najwa, I'm feeling it. I have been feeling it for so long. How do I actually get out of it?" is a question I get in various forms. And it's a question I absolutely love. This is what I say to you: Alongside

feeling the pain, there has to be acceptance of it. Acceptance of how it all happened. Acceptance of what you did. Acceptance of what they did. There has to be acceptance of the fact that you'll never again be the person you were before it happened. Acceptance of the scars it left on you. You need to transform those scars from being constant reminders of the pain into reminders of how far you've come from that pain. And, most important, there must be ownership on your part over your own life.

The tools in this room will be referred to as outlets, because they will offer you opportunities to plug into forgiveness and unplug from self-blame and attachment to past pain. If forgiveness is about letting go, it's about opening space for anything you're holding on to—feelings, thoughts, resentments, bitterness, helplessness—to be released.

OUTLET #1: STITCH YOUR SOUL WITH GOLD

You must let go of the idea that healing means going back to the person you were before the event that broke you. Many of us get so stuck on what we lost—and usually what we lost is not of monetary value. It could be years of our lives. It could be our innocence. It could be our self-confidence, our hope, our positive outlook. We get so focused on regaining what we lost because, to us, doing so is an indication we're on the right path. We get so focused on becoming the person we were before, but that's like trying to fit into a shell you've outgrown. The person you were is familiar. But do you see what direction you need to take to reach that person? It's in the past. It's behind you. So if that's what you're trying to do, I'm going to ask you kindly to stop.

You broke.
You were beautiful
before the break.
You were beautiful
as you were breaking.
You are beautiful
as you are reconstructing,
not unbreaking, yourself.
And, oh, how beautiful you will be
once you've stitched
the broken pieces of yourself
with the needle of self-love
and the golden thread of
home.

When you break, you can see all the parts of you that you needed to see. It's the messiest and most beautiful form of unraveling. You will be able to pick up each piece on its own, understand it, love it, be aware of it, and choose to place it within the new you. The gold you sew through your soul might look like scars, but remember that your scars are meant to remind you of how far you've come.

I'll give you an example of how I did this. When I described walking out of that office and not knowing which pain was the worst, my image of healing was going back to the woman I was before all that had happened. I was broken and looking to unbreak. But what I really needed to do was reconstruct. Because unbreaking meant wishing the pain away. And that's impossible. Reconstruction is an aware act. You can't build a home while blindfolding yourself. To reconstruct means to know all the parts, to know the purpose of each part and where to place it. On my journey of going back to understand why I became the person I was before the pain happened, I gave the parts of me an opportunity to be seen, heard, and loved by me. And it's not that I was abandoning my past self by making that decision. I was rebuilding her. I was learning about her. Now I *know* myself and I know how to be an active participant in my own life. For example, I know now that I'm an empath and that it was a big part of the reason why I felt the need to please. Wanting to go back to the person I was before would mean I'm asking to be someone whose empathy remains in the shadows, directing me to the wrong places. Reconstructing means I choose to keep that part of me, but now I know it. And I value it. Therefore I can build boundaries around that empathy.

I use the analogy of stitching because stitching is painful, as is healing. It takes time and effort. It requires forgiveness. It requires letting go. It requires taking leadership over your own life. And that will make you lose people. You might feel lonely. But, remember, you are building the most powerful person in your life—you. And that is the biggest win.

In the process of accepting there is no going back to the person you were before the painful or traumatic event, you are automatically separating your healing from an apology or an acknowledgment. You are taking ownership of this reconstruction. You are the builder.

In *Sparks of Phoenix*, I wrote:

> *The one who broke you*
> *cannot heal you.*

You must let go of the idea that you can heal only if the person who hurt you apologizes or regrets their actions. Instead of laying blame on them for your current situation, you must hold them accountable for their past actions and take ownership over your present situation. They don't get that kind of power. They don't get to hold you hostage to the pain they put you through. And here's a secret: Many times, they don't even feel they have that power. You give it to them in your own mind. You give it to them by getting stuck on the painful moments you think they caused. They didn't cause the pain. They woke it up within you. Don't get me wrong. I'm not saying you *chose* to feel pain as a result of their painful action. What I'm saying is that their power does not extend past that finite moment. Now the power is back to you.

Sometimes forgiving yourself takes the form of you
telling the story as you experienced it, not as someone else
wrote it. Instead of "He first did this, then this,
then that," you are saying "I did, I felt, I . . ."
And this is not to lay blame on you . . . it's to
make you the narrator of your own story.

OUTLET #2: USE "I" STATEMENTS

I learned so much of what I know today from teaching. As I was getting my teacher training, an early childhood education professor told us to encourage our students to use "I" statements, a term coined by the psychologist Thomas Gordon in the 1960s, when dealing with conflict resolution. I wondered why we weren't also taught this technique when it came to older students. For some reason, conflict resolution was considered important only in the very early years, whereas in older grades, the focus was more on classroom management and curriculum planning. And this course wasn't mandatory for all of us, so it helped me understand the lack of awareness many teachers display about conflict resolution. When conflict occurred among or between older students, the focus was usually not on the student, but rather on making the problem go away, which often involved reminding the student of which rule they broke and then giving them an appropriate consequence.

With younger students, we were taught more productive methods. For example, let's say I am teaching third grade, and Lara and Sandy are two students in my class. One day at recess, Lara comes to me with tears in her eyes, saying, "She hurt my feelings!" When I speak to Sandy, she says that Lara is annoying because she always gets upset when Sandy plays with someone else. Do you see what's happening here? Both Lara and Sandy are pointing to the faults in the other person. When I remind them both to use "I" statements, Lara is more likely to say:

I feel sad when Sandy doesn't play with me because it makes me feel left out.

And Sandy is more likely to say:

I feel angry when Lara tries to stop me from playing with my other friends, because I like playing with everyone.

You see, often we make another person's actions feel like a big looming cloud overhead because of what we make their actions say about ourselves. And the moment we can separate their actions from what we think they mean about us, we can understand ourselves better. And we can also understand the other person better. This is what happens when we use "I" statements.

My friend Sam, for example, reached out to me a day after she discovered that her live-in boyfriend of two years was sexting multiple other women. She was so hurt and kept saying, "I don't understand how he could have cheated on me like this! Why isn't he even trying to explain? Isn't he trying to fix this?" So I asked her to replace every question with an "I" statement.

Instead of saying "How could he have lied to me?" you say, "I feel hurt when someone lies to me, because it makes me feel like I'm not worthy of being told the truth."

Instead of saying "He's not even explaining why!" you say, "I feel sad when someone doesn't try to resolve an issue, because it makes me feel like I'm not worthy of being fought for."

The "I" statement has three elements:

I felt/feel _____ (insert emotion)

when _____ (recount the event that happened)

because _____ (insert what it made you think of)

When you are able to do that, you are able to take that last element—the "because"—and ask yourself if it is actually true. That's where your healing begins. You're healing not from the event, but instead from what it told you about yourself. And that lets you go back to the early moments in your life when that belief about yourself emerged. And, all of a sudden, your healing rises above that person and falls into you. And, now, instead of blaming that person for giving you the feeling of home and then taking it away, you start building your own home. So if you're in the process of building your own home, remember this. And if you've already built it, and now you're visiting the Forgiveness room, "I" statements will never fail you.

The goal of using an "I" statement is to steer away from "you" statements. "You" statements imply a state of homelessness, because you are trying to find the answer somewhere outside of yourself. The purpose of using "I" statements is to separate your healing from the person who caused you pain in any way. It's to drive you back to yourself. To your home.

Pillar #4: Forgiveness Is Not About Blame— It's About Letting Go

If there could be another name for this room, it would be letting go.

It doesn't matter who caused the pain or what led to it. What matters is that it affected you somehow. It's not like knowing who to blame is going to take the pain away. If anything, it only opens room for resentment. And that is such a heavy feeling to carry.

My pain lived on the surface. And no one told me they saw it until I opened up about it. The wound I'd been hiding for so long was under a Band-Aid. I was not allowing it to breathe, nor was I allowing it to turn into a scar, because I wasn't ready to let go. I wanted the wound to stay, to keep bleeding, so I could constantly give myself the right to feel the pain. So I could justify why I was in so much pain. Because how could I be in pain if it wasn't evident that I had a reason to be in pain, right? I held on to that identity of what happened to me so I could somehow keep reliving it and somehow feel alive. The hard part about letting go of the pain, of the event that taught me what I was believing about myself, was facing myself. And the truth of who I am.

Because if I don't have that pain to define me, who am I?

OUTLET #3: REDEFINE YOURSELF:
WHO ARE YOU WITHOUT THIS PAIN?

If you were to introduce yourself to someone right now, what would you say? (I will simplify this for you. Start with five words. Just five words.)

Before I came home to myself, I often introduced myself by what had happened to me. In my eyes, I was a victim of abuse. I was someone who experienced sexual harassment and power abuse. I was someone who wasn't heard. Someone fighting to be heard.

On my journey of coming home to myself, I changed the narrative. I am no longer defined by what happened to me, but by who I am. Now I would introduce myself as someone who's survived, who's rebuilt herself, who's reconstructed herself. I introduce myself as someone who's an active participant in her own life, not someone who had something done to her. Not someone who is reacting, but someone who is being.

It's hard for us to define ourselves without our pain, because all of a sudden we have to face the truth about ourselves. Most of us don't even know who we are. I'm not saying this to sound like I'm shaming you or myself for holding on to the pain. I'm simply trying to shed light on the reasons it's easier for us to live in pain than it is for us to live without pain. It's not because we want to live in pain. It's because living in pain is a lot less painful than living unanchored to something. To someone. To a memory. To a moment.

When we don't know who we are, we feel like we have no purpose. So we walk and live aimlessly, not feeling any sense of drive. Many of us would rather not live in that state of not knowing, so we go to what we know. Pain. We tell ourselves that carrying the identity of someone who experienced something is better than not carrying an identity at all.

Letting go is seeing and accepting yourself as you are, without the pain. Without the story. Without the labels. Without the identity you've created for yourself based on the pain or the story. Accepting that you are not what happened to you. And that you are not the result of it. Instead, you are who you are, with or without it. Does that mean that what happened to you wasn't bad enough? Or that it wasn't significant? Absolutely not.

OUTLET #4: CUT THE CORDS

In *Sparks of Phoenix*, I used the analogy of a marionette:

> *He attached strings to my self-worth*
> *and played with me*
> *like a marionette.*

If I could rewrite that poem, I'd say:

> *I attached my self-worth*
> *to his acceptance of me.*
> *I said, did, and felt*
> *what I thought I needed to say, do, and feel*
> *to be worthy of being loved, seen, and heard.*

STEP 1: Sit in silence.

STEP 2: Close your eyes or focus on one object.

STEP 3: Imagine a person who hurt you. Think of all the power you're giving them, as represented by the cords that tie you (the marionette) to them. Each cord represents something you can't let go of when it comes to that pain or that person.

STEP 4: Imagine picking up a pair of scissors. The scissors come directly from the foundation of your home. One blade is self-acceptance and one blade is self-awareness. You take the scissors to each cord separately and say *I accept you and I release you. You have no power over me.*

STEP 5: Every time you cut a cord, imagine its power flowing back into you. Into your heart. Into your home.

This activity is like saying *I am dismantling your power over me. The power that I thought was yours is now mine.*

Pillar #5: Forgiving Someone Does Not Grant Them Entry Back into Your Life, Including Your Past Self

The key phrase in this pillar is *including your past self.* Do you re-member the moment that I described sitting in that office with my superior at work and crying? That moment right there is where I got stuck for the next couple of years. Healing from the trauma—traumas—that occurred over the few years before that moment meant going back to that innocent unscathed girl who followed the rules perfectly. Who was on everyone's good side. Who was the one to be looked up to. I tried so hard to go back to being that girl that I broke even more.

It was like taking broken glass and trying to put it back exactly as it was before it broke. I needed to accept there was no going back to the person I was before. She was gone.

Remember when I told you I was facing the death of that woman I was convinced I needed to be to be happy? To be okay? Walk with me to the moment when I started accepting the need for that woman to die. One night, before my father took off on his yearly trip to Lebanon, I was sitting on the couch across from him in our living room, feeling like a lifeless body. My family didn't know what I was going through. They'd been witnessing me shrivel in every way possible, especially my mom, but they had no idea what was going on. I was so ashamed. So afraid.

For Father's Day, I'd shared a picture of me on Facebook holding his hand when I was one or two years old. I was wearing a white and red dress. My little blond curls were tied with cute red hair ties that looked like cherries. And I was smiling. You couldn't see my dad in that picture, but you could see my arm held up to hold his. My tiny little hand was grabbing on to his for dear life.

As my dad sat across from me, he said something in words I haven't memorized exactly, but I remember them. My dad, a man of very few words, said: "You know that picture you shared? When you were that small, I used to look in your eyes and say 'This girl is going places.' Because of the look that you had in your eyes. And now that look is gone."

That night, I looked at myself in the mirror. And cried. And cried. And cried. I couldn't recognize myself. I felt I was looking at a stranger. I was looking at a sky, choking, not knowing whether it was going to rain or let the sun strike through.

I could see what my dad was saying. I was no longer me. I was in transition between who I was and who I needed to become. And my body couldn't accept either version of myself, so I just became an empty shell, desperately gasping for any ray of life to inhabit me. I was homeless.

To become who I was meant to become, I needed to stop trying to be who I had been. The woman I used to be based her worth on building temporary homes in other people. The woman I wanted to be knew that her own home within was the only home she needed.

I needed to stop wishing away the pain. I needed to stop waiting for an apology. I needed to stop waiting for an acknowledgment of the pain. I needed to stop feeling so small next to those in positions of power. Most of all, I needed to stop wishing myself away by feeling ashamed of wanting to feel home. I needed to forgive myself first. I needed to acknowledge myself. I needed to feel home on my own. I needed to stop waiting for someone to fight for me. I needed to stop waiting for someone to give me a voice. So I fought for myself. And I raised my own voice.

In hindsight, that moment with my tears falling on my lap in my superior's office was the moment I started grieving the death of the past me. And started building a home within myself.

After this story, I realized that holding on to what happened to me was never going to bring me healing. Dwelling on why my superior didn't stand up for me or validate how bad my experience was, was only further alienating me from my own home within. When you are wronged, all you want is for that wrong to be taken away. And I relied on a system of power to give me power, when what I needed to do was never accept my credibility's being dependent on a system of power to validate it. I didn't need an investigation finding to prove to me that I lived what I know I lived.

Forgiving them . . . all of them . . . meant I had to let go of what was out of my control. Forgiving them meant taking my time to get to where I could dissociate what they did to me from who I am. Forgiving them could not have happened without me forgiving myself for putting so much emphasis on others' validation of my pain. Forgiving myself and forgiving them put the power over my life back in my hands. It empowered me to say *I am not who you say I am. I am who I am. My truth is not dependent on whether you see it as truth. My truth is dependent on the truth I know I lived.*

The following outlet will help you reach the same level of liberty.

OUTLET #5: AS YOU LEAVE THIS ROOM, AFFIRM

By forgiving, I am letting go of what I have no control over.

I can only control my thoughts, my feelings, and my actions (what I do with my thoughts and feelings).

I get to decide when and who I forgive.

I forgive myself.

I can't rush forgiveness.

It is my choice whether that person can or can't come into my life again.

To end this chapter, I want to share with you a poem I started writing in a moment where I caught myself wishing the pain away. Upon applying the knowledge I've acquired on authentic forgiveness, I was able to steer my feelings toward acceptance.

I wish I could go back
to the exact moment
before the moment I met you.
To turn around
and sit one seat over
from the seat where I sat
the night I met you.
I wish I could go back to
the exact moment
before the moment I walked out my door
that night.
To turn around and do anything.
Anything at all.
Except for walk out the door.
I wish I could go back
to the exact moment
before the moment
I smiled when you said hello.
Because for the longest time, I thought my smile
invited you to say hello.
And that my hello

invited you to say
all the words you'd say
to draw me in
like a butterfly to a raging fire
that looked like rays of sun.
I wish I could go back
to the exact moment
before every moment
I said yes
when I wanted to say no.
To remind myself that
if being loved was dependent
on me breaking into pieces,
I can choose to keep myself together.
I wish I could go back to the exact moment
before every moment
that I chose to say
what you wanted to hear.
To remind myself that
if being heard was dependent
on me being silent,
I can choose to let my voice roar.
Oh how I wish . . .
I could go back.
But oh how grateful I am
that my wish never came true.
Because in this exact moment
I am who I am,
I am where I am,

because of every moment
before every exact moment
that I fell to ashes
only to rise
with gold-stitched wings
and a voice so powerful,
even I can't ignore it.

FOUR

Compassion

In a world full of judgment and division, this room is here to remind you of three kinds of compassion: compassion toward the world, compassion toward yourself, and compassion from others. This is the only room in your home where people are allowed in. And this act of welcoming others into your home inherently involves boundaries.

It's essential for you to show compassion toward yourself and the world. And with that same level of compassion, you must be selective with whom you welcome into your home. Just as you display your compassion to the world through empathy and a desire to help, so should the people you welcome into your home. They should have the ability to feel with you, not for you.

Are you ready to start learning about the power you have over who walks into your home?

Let's walk in.

I am recalling a memory from when I was in fourth grade. I was eight years old.

> *Our reading lesson was about a heart surgeon who innovated a procedure that would save thousands of patients from dying. I remember being so fascinated by how much good this doctor did for the world. And I kept imagining how much reward he deserved for saving lives.*
>
> *I remember, innocent little me, running to my teacher at the end of the period with so much admiration for the doctor, and asking my teacher if he was going to heaven because he'd saved so many lives. And my smile quickly faded when she said, "No. Because he's not Muslim. He's going to hell."*
>
> *I remember going home with so much sadness in my heart. I couldn't comprehend how someone who's done so much good could not go to heaven. I'd grown up listening to beautiful stories about religion from my grandma, and I was taught by her never to judge anyone by anything other than their actions.*
>
> *I went to my dad and told him what had happened. And I remember him telling me, "It's not up to us to judge where anyone is going. Only God knows what's in a person's heart."*

If this story isn't evidence enough for you that children are born as blank canvases that we end up conditioning to see the world through labels, I don't know what is. I was feeling sad because I couldn't stand the thought that someone out there would go to hell simply because they weren't Muslim. Can you imagine the person I would be today if I hadn't gone home and told this story to my dad? Or if my dad had confirmed what the teacher said? Can you imagine the person I would be today if I'd just believed what my teacher told me that day and walked through life believing that the separation between going to heaven and hell has to do with what religion you say you believe in? I would have continued judging people based on labels and not empathizing with them in any way. I would have allowed my judgment of them to override my empathy.

I was fortunate to have parents who taught me a version of faith that was very kind, compassionate, and empathetic. It was a version that respects people's freedom of choice and their actions more than the labels they identify with.

A few times in my childhood, my dad would take me to visit his friends in nearby villages who were Christians and Druze. A conversation we always had on our way there and back was that the most important thing is that a person is a good person. Their actions and manners mattered more than their religious identities.

My image of God was that of light. I didn't follow the rules because I worried about going to hell. I followed them because I loved the image of God that I saw—fair, just, understanding, empathetic—a version that conflicted with the one I was taught at the Islamic school I attended. My dad always urged me to tell him anything I learned in school so he could correct it for me.

You see, my problem wasn't with God. My problem was with what people told me about God. When I was in university, that same kind of heaven-and-hell, black-and-white judgmental version of religion was practiced among many of those I was surrounded with. I had people tell me that if I entered a room with my left foot, the angels wouldn't greet me. If I wore makeup, my prayer wouldn't be valid. If I wore nail polish, I couldn't properly cleanse myself before I prayed.

I just remember thinking *Why would God care if I wore nail polish when I pray? Why would God care if I entered a room with my right foot or my left foot?* And are those minor insignificant details, in my view, more important than actually being a good person? Like I'd see all these girls around me (remember I had no guy friends because that was frowned upon) being all devout in public, but I knew they were in relationships behind their parents' backs. I knew they would gossip about other girls. And among many other things, I witnessed them being judgmental toward others for the same things they did in private. To me, those things were worse than wearing nail polish while I prayed.

My image of God was that of compassion toward everyone, not just those who identify as Muslims. God tells me to see people for who they really are, not all the labels that surround them. And that's the kind of compassion I treat the world with. When someone speaks negatively to me or anyone else, I always reflect on whether they had the same upbringing I had. Did they have a dad like mine who corrected what their school indoctrinated them to believe? Did they have a mom like mine who always pushed me to look at people's actions before looking at their labels? And I do my best to keep that in mind as I respond. I'm not perfect, but I always try my best to show compassion in my responses.

I will share my story of taking my hijab off in detail in Chapter Five, Clarity. For the purposes of this Compassion room, I want to discuss how compassion played a role in that part of my life. I took my hijab off in July of 2018. When I publicized my decision,

I received quite a bit of hatred. I shared this experience on social media a few days after I went public with my decision:

> The last few days have been really tough on me. The amount of hatred I've been receiving is too much for even mountains to carry. I've even responded in ways that don't resemble me, because of how overwhelming the negativity has become.
>
> If you are judging me or what's in my heart based on only what you see, go ahead. I can't stop you. If you want to unfollow me, go ahead and unfollow me. But I will not change. And my message will not change. My heart will not change.
>
> I will never judge a person by what they say they believe, only by their actions, by their hearts, and by their conscience. By the good they bring to this world. That's what my faith teaches me. So don't put words in my mouth and don't give yourself the right to make assumptions about me or why I do what I do.
>
> Peace and love to you, even if you hate me. Peace and love to you.

Why am I sharing this with you? Because it is a perfect example of me practicing self-compassion while expressing my understanding of compassion toward others. Instead of allowing people's opinions of me to make me feel less of myself, I chose to speak to myself with compassion, empathy, and a willingness to help myself rise.

Pillar #1: Self-Compassion Sets the Bar for Compassion from Others

Being at home with yourself does not mean you are unaffected by the world around you. Practicing self-compassion will prepare you for the kind of compassion you will accept from outsiders. In the process, you will learn how to build boundaries around your home. Being at home with yourself means knowing who to welcome into your home, under what conditions, and when it's time for them to leave. That's why it's important for you to learn how to build boundaries for all the visitors who attempt to enter your home. Did you notice how I used *build* instead of *draw*? It's like building a fence around your home or putting a lock on your door. And part of that process is understanding what kind of compassion you deserve.

This ties back directly to self-love. Spending time to learn how to be self-compassionate and practicing self-compassion is not selfish. The time you take to be compassionate with yourself is not taking away from your compassion for others. In fact, it's ensuring that when you are compassionate with others, you aren't doing so by depleting yourself, that you're not developing resentment. It ensures that your compassion is coming from a healthy place.

It used to be that when I experienced any kind of problem, I'd look at other, bigger problems in the world and say *But my problem is nothing compared to that. I'd better be grateful for not having to go through that.* I'd think of the millions who live in poverty, or war victims. With time, I realized that being compassionate with others does not require you to minimize your own problems. You can be both at the same time. You can do the best you can to effect change for others while also making change for yourself.

Plus, it's not okay to be compassionate toward others only out of pity or feeling superior to them because they suffer or struggle more than you do. That's sympathy, not empathy. Empathy requires you to feel *with*, not *for*, the other person. And just as I wouldn't want others to feel pity for me, I need to feel empathy *with* myself, not pity *for* myself.

Pillar #2: Welcome Those Who've Earned the Right to Be Welcomed

As much as I want to tell you that being at home with yourself requires you to stand tall on your own without ever asking anyone for help, I'd be lying if I said so. Allowing people into your life doesn't take away from your at-homeness. But this doesn't mean you welcome anyone and everyone. It's essential to be selective with the visitors who knock on your door. Those visitors are not limited to people; their opinions are sometimes visitors, too. As can be cultural and religious norms.

So how do you know who to welcome into your home?

I call the strategies in this room binding blocks, because they serve as tools to build connections with others.

The first binding block is the most important.

BINDING BLOCK #1: REMEMBER YOU'RE THE HOST

Before you focus on who to welcome into the Compassion room, welcome yourself. Remember that you are the owner of this home. You are the host. Be compassionate with yourself. Put yourself in your own shoes. Grow the desire to help yourself. If you were to host a dinner at your home, you probably would get so caught up in serving everyone on your guest list that you would forget you are the host. It's important that you have your name on the guest list and that you take time to join in sharing the food you made. It's also important that you place yourself up there with those you love. Remember that the process of building a home for yourself is about you. It's about your having a place to come home to at the end of the day, before you feel the need to go to someone else. So make sure your home welcomes you before it welcomes anyone else.

The people you welcome into your home, who you allow to sit at your table, are those who will listen without judgment, without the immediate need to respond, criticize, or analyze. Those who practice, not just show, compassion. Those who, even when they disapprove of your actions or what led you here, will tell you "It must be so hard. I can't begin to imagine feeling what you're feeling." Not people who will say things like "But how did you not see this or that?" or any statement that makes you feel your problem is nothing compared to what they or others are going through.

The people you can trust with parts of your story are those who've earned your trust. Would you freely share your thoughts and ideas with anyone out there, knowing that they might steal them, not listen, or simply not care? No, you wouldn't. So stop welcoming those people into your home!

Would you want the people you welcome into your home to feel bad for you? Or would you want them to see you and be there for you out of genuine love? Welcome those you know will feel *with* you, in empathy, not bad *for* you. Empathy is an integral part of compassion. Welcome those who won't sit there and compare their problems to yours. Those who will give you advice when you ask for it. Those who will amplify your voice when it feels so faint. Those who will remind you of your value when you forget it. Those who will remind you of your logic when you are so far gone past your ability to assess your situation in an unbiased manner because of being enmeshed in it.

The first comment I usually get when I open up to a friend about something I'm going through is "Why didn't you tell me?!" And even though I know that they mean well, the last thing I need to do is explain why I didn't speak earlier. The last thing I need to do is defend my trust for them, our friendship, or what they mean to me. That adds an extra burden on me. And deters me from even beginning to share, because I know what that would entail. It would feel like I'm carrying both the burden of the story and the burden of validating the person I'm opening up to.

Even though I was aching to speak to someone about what I was going through when I was breaking out of the shell of the woman I thought I needed to be, my first instinct was to tell myself *They won't understand. So I'd better stay quiet. They'll ask me why I didn't come to them any sooner. But before that, they'll say something that will make me question myself . . . how could I not have known any better?*

The friends who fell out of my life were the ones who listened to my pain and agony with judgment rather than empathy, with a desire to feel better about themselves by belittling me. Those are people I don't speak to anymore. I don't invite them into my home anymore. It doesn't mean that they are bad people—they're just not people who've earned their welcome into my home. If they knock on the door, I might hear what they have to say. But I treat them just as I treat my emotions, as visitors.

What if I've already welcomed people into my home who have treated
me that way? What do I do now?

BINDING BLOCK #2: WRITE OUT
YOUR GUEST LIST

Imagine you're hosting a gathering. You've invited your closest
friends and prepared mounds of food. Think of the guest list—who
is on it? Write those names down and come back to this.

Would you invite someone who deeply hurt you or a friend of
yours to the gathering? Would you welcome them—or any stranger
off the street—into your home? Probably not. So why do you allow
those who have hurt you to get to you? Why do you give their opinions a place to rest their feet?

~

Sometimes people walk in wearing a cloak of compassion
that you soon realize is not real. When this happens,
remember you're the owner of your home. You may escort
them out the door just as you escorted them in.

~

If someone you invited over for dinner insulted you or disrespected you, what would you do? Wouldn't you kindly ask them to
leave and, if required, have someone help you escort them out? And
even if you patiently got through the evening with them, would you
invite them again? Exactly. Having people in your life who don't

show true compassion toward you is no different. And don't say you don't have a choice. You do.

I always thought my ability to be that kind, patient, understanding person who made excuses for people made me a good person. I was the type who always believed people can change. That everyone deserved a second, third, tenth chance if they really wanted to change. And it took me years to understand that that "type" stemmed from my empathy. And nothing was wrong with that. But I always ended up resenting those who hurt me, even though I had every opportunity to say no, to end my relationship or communication with them, or to stop interacting with them at all. But I chose to continue. I ended up resenting them for taking advantage of my empathy without taking responsibility for my own acceptance of their behavior. This would lead me to judge myself for feeling resentful, which would tempt me to apologize to them for saying things I said while I was reacting or responding. And the cycle would go on. Why?

Because I had no boundaries. I didn't even know what boundaries were. But, oh, how wrong I was. I've already spoken about boundaries in the Self-Love room, but it applies here as well. I didn't grow up seeing my mom, bless her heart, ever say *no* to anyone. She always did the best she could to be there for everyone. But that came at a cost. That cost was herself. In the past, I always thought the biggest honor would be to become like her, but now that I'm aware of how self-destructive pleasing everyone around you is, I know the importance of boundaries. I now know that putting myself first doesn't make me a bad person.

People shouldn't feel so comfortable taking you for granted. They shouldn't believe you won't take away the privilege of being welcomed into your life. So how do you decide who to welcome into your home? Building boundaries will help you set the criteria for who you allow in and who you keep at the door. Boundaries are as important in any relationship with others as a protective fence around your home or a lock on your door. You get to decide who to allow in, who to keep in, and who to ask to leave. You get to decide how frequently to invite someone or whether not to invite them anymore.

Also remember this: It's not only people that will visit your home. Their opinions are visitors, too. Even though we might not allow certain people into our life, we still allow their opinions of us to affect us. It's important to be aware that people's influence on our life often surpasses their physical presence in our life.

Take stock of the thoughts and opinions on your guest list. It's a powerful way of thinking about other people's opinions, isn't it?

And it's not just specific people's opinions of you that affect your life. Societal pressures, religious standards, and cultural boundaries also affect you. For example, a woman's body shape, weight, and physical features are highly scrutinized by society and judged by a set of unspoken norms. Social media outlets reinforce these norms. When you allow those unspoken norms to dictate how you see yourself, you're allowing society's ideals into your home, even if you reject those ideals on a conscious level.

Here's how you can set boundaries for letting such unspoken rules into your home through social media:

1. Unfollow social media accounts that preach those unspoken rules. Stop your intentional exposure to them.

2. Prepare yourself for dealing with unintentional exposure to them. For example, you can choose the option to "hide similar

posts"; leave a comment kindly expressing your opinion; or just keep scrolling and not give the post any attention. Are there any other ways you can see yourself preparing for these instances?

I still allowed those who judged me into my life without really welcoming them. How? By allowing their opinions of me to affect the way I saw myself. If I had imagined welcoming them only if they came in compassionately, I wouldn't have welcomed them in the first place. Examples of these times are when I chose to take off my hijab. When I moved out of my parents' home. When I embraced my own way of dressing. They felt like unwelcome guests that were just there.

Pillar #3: Build Boundaries Before Allowing People into Your Home

When I was first introduced to boundaries I had no idea what they were. I thought a boundary had to do with me setting certain standards to change the other person's behavior. I thought that it was a set of standards that, if someone broke them with me, they'd be in trouble. However, time and wisdom taught me I could never, and should never aim to, change another person's behavior. A boundary has nothing to do with other people. It has everything to do with me.

Simply put, building boundaries is about saying *This is what I accept, and this is what I don't accept.*

You don't build a boundary in the face of someone else, you build a boundary around yourself—one that honors the value you know you have within you. Putting up walls in reaction to what someone says or does is operating from a place of fear. A boundary, on the other hand, is about you honoring and valuing what you have inside your home.

Here is another powerful way to visualize boundaries: Imagine having jewels and diamonds inside your home. It's not a boundary to say *I want to protect these from people stealing them.* Setting a boundary is saying *These are valuable, and if someone tries to wear them without my permission, I will not accept that.* That's the difference between defense mode and response mode.

∽

Do not constantly walk through life in defense mode.
When your boundaries are violated, respond. Do not react.

∽

Many of us make the mistake of believing that setting a boundary ends at expressing to someone that one of their actions hurts us. After that, we depend on the person's own conscience to say *I'd better stop doing that.* If by expressing your boundary to someone, you are expecting that their behavior will change, that is not a boundary. A boundary is free of the expectation that it will change a person's behavior. That's a choice they have to make. When you attach the validity of the boundary to the person's changed behavior, you are stepping into that person's home and defining your worth based on their treatment of you.

When you focus the boundary on yourself, your focus shifts from feeling hurt because someone is not giving you the value you think you deserve to seeing that this person is violating the standard of respect you set for yourself. And you say *My worth is not dependent on someone respecting how I want to be treated.*

꩜

Part of respecting others is respecting their boundaries.
Part of respecting yourself is building your own boundaries.

꩜

Instead of asking *Why are they continuing to hurt me when I've already expressed that what they're doing hurts me?*, start asking *Do I accept this in my life? I do not accept disrespect. I do not accept inconsistency in communication. I do not accept someone treating me in a way that makes me see their clear lack of respect for me as a human.* You are not basing the validity of your boundary on someone else respecting it or not. You are taking your power over valuing your own worth. That boundary speaks of that value. Binding Block #3 will go into detail about how to do this.

We spoke about this in the Forgiveness room: Once you start using "I" statements, your whole life will change. When you take ownership over what you do, how you feel, and how you think, that's when you begin to change. That's when you dismantle the power of any person external to you over you. Their actions are only powerful over you, your well-being, your thoughts and feelings if you allow them that power.

"But it still hurts me when people do something that they know hurts me." That's a comment I frequently receive. And this is my response: Imagine that you're walking outside and it unexpectedly starts raining. You will get wet. But it's up to you to decide whether you're going to walk away from the rain and go to somewhere you can dry yourself, or continue standing in the rain because . . . you're already wet. In the Surrender room, there's a powerful analogy about how our hearts adapt to their context, which is exactly the same as saying I'm already wet. For now, think of being hit by unexpected rain. It's surprising. You don't know what to do or how to react. Think about the power of taking a step back and, instead of dwelling on what happened and why, you think *What do I do now? This* (whatever that boundary violation was) *happened. It hurt. But I have a choice. What do I want to do now?*

You know what many people do? What I've done? And what you've probably done? When we accept a boundary violation once, when it happens again, we accept it, because we've accepted it before. It's familiar. We know how it will go. We know we can survive it. We know that, on some level, speaking up might cause the person who crossed our boundary to walk away. So we allow them to stomp over that boundary just so they stay. Something else you may have done is tell them that the way you feel is a result of the way they're treating you. We frequently try to change others' behavior by guilting them. For example, in moments of conflict, we say things like *I can't believe you make me feel this way. I don't deserve this. This is not fair.* In moments like this, I want you to remember to use your "I" statements. Your feeling better is not dependent on the other person's changing their behavior. It's dependent on you not accepting the behavior after you've expressed where you stand on it.

BINDING BLOCK #3: BUILD
YOUR BOUNDARIES

STEP 1: Learn about yourself. Know your value. The foundation of your home and the Self-Love room will help with this immensely. Boundaries are a reflection of the value you see in yourself.

STEP 2: Set boundaries using "I" statements. Even though your boundaries are based on you, they will look and sound different in different contexts—for example, with friends, family, your religious or cultural community, co-workers, strangers, and so on. The bottom line is, you reserve the right to enforce a strong protective fence around your home. You reserve the right to have a lock on your front door. You reserve the right to remove anyone who breaks in through the window or walks in without knocking.

Here are some examples of what boundaries might look like:

1. I will end the conversation with someone who constantly interrupts me.

2. I will say no when I'm uncomfortable.

3. I will leave the room when X yells at me.

4. I will limit the time and energy I spend on those who try to shame me through religion.

5. I will not tolerate anyone's behavior or words just because I'm afraid of hurting their feelings if I ask them to stop.

6. I will not do or say anything that diminishes my self-respect just to make someone else feel better about themselves.

7. Add your own examples . . .

STEP 3: Reinforce your boundaries. Express your boundaries when you need to. Again, some people will adapt to your boundaries through common sense and through sensing your level of comfort. But some people need to have those boundaries explicitly made clear.

STEP 4: Stick to your word. Not sticking to your word would be like adjusting the fence you've built around your home based on how high or low the person is willing jump. For example, if your partner yells at you and you state that if they do that again, you will end the relationship, but they continue to do that and you stay, you are not honoring your own boundary. And this is not to say that their choice to mistreat you is your fault. Not at all. But your sticking to your boundary is a direct reflection of how secure you are in your worth. If you're afraid that your partner will leave, you'll continue to lower that boundary and feel a mix of fear, dependence, resentment, and helplessness. You'll adapt your boundary to their level of willingness to respect it. For example, you might say something like *At least don't yell at me around my family*.

The less you think of your worth, the lower your boundaries are going to be, and the less powerful and strong you're going to feel about them. If you believe you deserve less, you won't know how to set a boundary. You won't know what not to accept in your life.

That knowledge and awareness of yourself is a direct reflection of the boundary you'll build.

And if you're beating yourself up over already accepting poor treatment, don't continue to accept it by telling yourself *I'm already wet*. Rather, make a trip to the Forgiveness room and forgive yourself. Make a trip to the Self-Love room and love your authentic self. Make a trip to the Surrender room and feel your emotions. Make a trip to the Clarity room and see yourself. Come back here and promise yourself to reinforce your boundaries moving forward.

Remember your guest list. Who would you allow into your home? Is it those who'll jump the fence and sneak in without knocking on the door and being welcomed? An essential part of being home is welcoming those who respect your boundaries without making your boundaries about them, but about you. People in your home have the access and ability to violate your boundaries, but sometimes they choose not to out of genuine respect for you. This is where you have to decide who to keep inside and who to evict.

Every time I share the necessity of building boundaries, I get questions that are derivatives of "But what if it's your own family? What if it's your work? . . ." In other words, "What if the people I need to build boundaries with are too close or an integral part of my life?" It's a lot easier to build boundaries with people you don't have any kind of history with or attachment to.

I have a story to tell you. When I first started showing a bit of my hair, I attended a family dinner. All the aunts, uncles, and their children were there. One of my aunts, in front of everyone, said to me, in a way to shame me: "So, are you happy with yourself?"

I remember feeling a rush of blood to my face. Everyone around us heard her. There were a few moments of silence in the room.

My cousins looked away. At this point in my life, I had a lot more courage and willingness not to please than I ever did before. In that moment, reverting to my past ways of pleasing meant I would just be quiet and dwell in my own shame. But this time, I spoke up. I said to her: "Yes, I am." In the past, this would have been considered so disrespectful. The past me would have said *My aunt's older than me. She's older, period. I need to respect her no matter what.* But the present me said *Respecting others should never come at the expense of you disrespecting yourself.*

After this incident, I didn't speak to my aunt. Months later, she told my sister to apologize to me on her behalf. I told my sister to tell her I accepted the apology and that I never wanted to hear that kind of comment again. And I never did.

The following script might help you with your family members:

> *I know you believe that you are coming from a place of love and protection, but you have to respect my autonomy. Loving me should not be conditional on whether I do or say what you approve of. You might think shaming me will protect me, but it will only hold me back from being my own person. I am human. I will make mistakes. It doesn't make me a bad . . . [daughter, son, . . .].*

The workplace can also be a touchy area in which to set boundaries. Especially if someone holds power over you, you might feel like you don't want to upset them or be on their bad side. And, especially as an empath, you will feel not pleasing someone isn't something you can stand. Here is what I will remind you of: *You are not a bad person for not accepting someone taking advantage of you or your time.*

You must stand up for yourself. And if that means saying no, or "That is not part of my job," that's okay. Reporting inappropriate behavior or harassment is part of building boundaries as well. The bottom line is, fairness and equitable opportunities at your workplace should never be at the cost of you pleasing others. And it should definitely never be conditional on your accepting any kind of disrespect or unfair treatment.

Pillar #4: Part of Self-Compassion Is Building Boundaries Around Your Emotions

Emotions are visitors in your home. In *The Nectar of Pain*, I wrote:

> *If pain built a home in*
> *your heart,*
> *remember that it has*
> *doors.*
> *And it has*
> *windows.*
> *Open the windows to*
> *allow happiness in.*
> *Better yet, open the doors and*
> *walk outside.*

If you're at a point where you feel like you know your value (the value of what's in your home), but when negative emotions visit you (discussed further in Chapter Six, "Surrender"), they push you to cling to people for validation that you're worthy, or to seek refuge in other people's homes, here is what I want you to remember: *Even*

though it's crucial for you to be aware of the emotions that visit you,
it's also necessary for you to not give them a permanent spot inside your
home. Remember, you are in control—not the emotion.

So, even if those emotions (shame, guilt, embarrassment, and so
on) don't permanently belong in your home, plan for what to do
when they visit you. What boundaries do you build there? What's the
thought process that would make a visiting negative emotion, such
as *Something is wrong with me (shame)*, leave? Do you just ignore it?
If you just ignore emotions because you want to numb yourself and
not feel their pain, that pain piles up over time. The goal is to get to a
point where you can say to pain *I welcome you. I hear what you're tell-*
ing me about myself. I acknowledge where it's coming from. I know that
nothing is wrong with me. I have made mistakes but that doesn't mean
something is fundamentally wrong with me. Now you can leave.

The problem many of us live with is that over the years, we've
gotten used to certain emotions being permanent occupants of our
home. Part of our learning boundaries with other people is learning to extract the occupants that are already in our home—our
emotions—and question their presence. For example, my feelings
of worthlessness and isolation were always inside of me. But they
didn't stem from nowhere. And I didn't learn about building boundaries with others until I could tell those occupants that all they told
me about myself wasn't true. That is how I was able to see my value
(Step 1 in Binding Block #3).

∽

Emotions are visitors, not occupants, of your home.
Separate yourself from your emotions.

∽

If certain emotions have been actual occupants in your home and you just became aware of them as a result of tracing back your *Why can't I have that?* story, now is the time for you to walk over to the Surrender room and give those emotions an outlet to be felt.

You have to make space inside yourself for new emotions to come in. How about we replace shame with self-love? And guilt with self-forgiveness? And not feeling good enough with feeling content with who we are? The opposites cannot exist within you at the same time, so which do you choose? You have to make space for the choice you made. You can't stock a refrigerator with fresh food if it's full of old, expired products. First you have to throw out the old stuff. You can't place new books you want to read on a bookshelf stuffed with old books you've already read. Can you?

Pillar #5: Believe You're Worthy of What People Have to Offer You

Before you welcome people into your home, truly believe you are worthy of what they have to offer you. When you don't know what you deserve, you're more likely to welcome anyone who knocks on your door, because you equate someone knocking on your door with your door's worthiness of being knocked on. When you develop self-compassion, you're not standing on the side of the street asking anyone to come into your home. Instead, you're safe and secure inside your home, deciding whether to welcome whoever knocks on the door.

One time, I was speaking to Stephan, a new friend of mine who is a wildly successful speaker. He was helping me set up my speaking topics and my pitches for speakers' bureaus. One of the first things he asked me was, "What are you open to receiving?"

"Open to receiving?" I asked, thinking to myself *What does that even mean?!*

Stephan proceeded to say, "You can tell me that you're willing to receive five speaking engagements a year or a hundred speaking engagements a year . . . forty thousand dollars a year or five hundred thousand dollars a year. But are you ready and open to receiving that kind of money? Do you genuinely believe that you deserve it? Because that makes all the difference."

Naturally, tears were streaming down my face.

I didn't know what I deserved. At that point in my life, I was more likely to dwell on what I didn't get without ever expressing that I wanted to get it. Let's apply this to welcoming people into your life. When you don't know what you're open to receiving, you will take in anything and later realize that it's too little or simply not what you want. But when you take the time to know what you want, you will be open and ready to receive it.

I always felt like a burden when someone offered to do something for me. I felt bad that they had to exert that kind of effort just to make things easier for me. But that stemmed from my not knowing that sometimes people express their love through effort, through action, and that I was worth that effort and action! I'll give you an example. Adam, the guy who I will tell you more about in the Surrender room, lives an hour's drive away from me, in another city. The first few times we met, he drove to a park near me and we would go for long walks. Every time I would suggest meeting halfway or driving to his city, he would say, "I know you're exhausted from writing and I wouldn't want you to exhaust yourself more by driving. I have the time. So let me come to you." This guy, on top of already driving two hours a day to get to his work, would drive an extra two hours just to see me. And

I felt so bad to the point where I would feel bad for wanting to see him because I knew it entailed two extra hours of driving for him.

After reflecting on my conversation with Stephan, I realized I felt bad because I wasn't willing to receive someone else's expression of love for me. Because I didn't truly believe that I deserved it. I blinded myself to my worthiness of what others had to offer me because of what I believed about myself. So after a few times, I stopped feeling bad. And I turned it into saying, "I appreciate that you've driven this long to see me. Thank you."

Sometimes, people just want to give us love, time, attention, and affection because they genuinely see us for who we are. And they're willing to give all that to us compassionately. And it's our own rejection of ourselves and what we deserve that makes us believe that what they're giving us is too much.

You'll read this again in the Surrender room, but it applies here as well: It takes time to accept more than scraps when you believe that it's too much for you. What's wrong with someone actually making you a priority in their life? What's wrong with someone putting in the effort to show you their love? You deserve that. It's not too much. It's the bare minimum that you deserve from someone you're welcoming into your home.

BINDING BLOCK #4: BE OPEN TO RECEIVING FROM OTHERS COMPASSIONATELY

The next time someone offers you something and your first instinct is to say no, reflect on whether you're saying no because you genuinely don't want what they're offering or because you don't believe you deserve what they're offering you.

It's easy to become cynical about what people have to offer you when all you've known is being given too little. I realized that I'd focused too much on all the people who weren't there for me during my hard times—those who I trusted who judged me instead of showing me their compassion when I needed it most. I accepted that what they had to offer me was the most I could ever get. After all, they were the closest to me. They knew me. That blinded me to what others had to offer me. It pushed me to make the blanket statement that I couldn't trust anyone. If those closest to me betrayed me that way, how could anyone else be any different?

For those, I wrote:

> *To all the people I pushed away while I was healing:*
> *Forgive me for not being able to*
> *welcome you*
> *when I really wanted to.*
> *I was scared.*
> *I was scared*
> *you'd judge me.*
> *I was scared*
> *you wouldn't understand.*
> *I was scared*
> *you'd ask me how I couldn't have known better.*
> *I was scared*
> *you'd push me away*
> *and remind me of all the reasons*
> *I don't deserve to be loved.*
> *I was scared.*
> *Everyone I welcomed before you*

either lied
or left
or took more than what I had to give.
Everyone I welcomed before you
only stayed as long as I was who they wanted me to be
instead of who I actually am.
I'm sorry I made you feel I couldn't trust you
when the truth was I couldn't even trust myself.

As we end this chapter, I want you to remember this: Asking yourself if someone is entering your home with compassion before you allow them in will save you so much heartache.

If someone doesn't believe you, does that show compassion? No. So why would you allow them into your life?

If someone isn't standing by you, does that show compassion? No. So why would you allow them into your life?

If someone disrespected you, hurt you, lied to you, lied about you, or made up rumors about you, does that show compassion? No. So why would you allow them into your life?

FIVE

Clarity

∾

The purpose of the Clarity room is to get you to see yourself clearly. You will remove the layers that stand in the way of you seeing yourself. The more time you spend in this room, the clearer your vision, in every sense of the word, becomes.

You enter this room when you can't make sense of what you're going through, when you're feeling confused. During a trying time of your life, you might find yourself here on most days. Other times, once you get some clarity, you might feel the need to spend time in other rooms. Most of us look to others for clarity. We try to see our own truths through the eyes of others. In this room, you will look through your own eyes, because that is the most important kind of clarity. It allows you to see who you are and what you stand for.

As you deconstruct who you were taught to be and unveil your authentic self, different mirrors in this room will reflect to you emotions that may be clouding your vision, such as anger and guilt.

Are you ready to turn your confusion into clarity?

Let's walk in.

I n the Clarity room, I see mirrors all around. In this room, there is no hiding from all the truths and stories of who you really are. I have a tendency to look in the mirror when I'm feeling confusion or that I'm losing myself. It brings me to tears sometimes and makes me feel like the queen of the world at others.

We often complain about not feeling seen for who we really are, but my belief is that the biggest loss is when we don't see ourselves clearly. Here, I'll first be sharing with you what the mirrors in the Clarity room have done for me. Then, to help you find your authentic self in this room, I'll be giving you specific strategies I'm calling mirrors. These mirrors offer a reflective process in which you can be real, raw, and authentic with yourself. That's the only way to achieve clarity.

There are layers around the core of who you really are that stop you from seeing yourself clearly. Those layers obscure your authentic self. They include who you think you should be and who you think you shouldn't be. And what stands in the way of who you really are and who you think you should be is your own fear that you aren't good enough. Fear creates a blur that stands in the way of seeing yourself clearly.

When you try so hard to become who you think you should be, and to avoid who you think you shouldn't be, you live a life that seems like an act. You master the art of hiding your authentic self. And if you do this long enough, you lose track of who you actually are. You lose your ability to be authentically present in your life. It's what happens with the mentality of "fake it till you make it." Some of us get so stuck in faking it that we actually forget who we really are. Until it's too late . . . when we've reached the end of our life, looking back at the life we wish we had lived.

As I urge you in the Dream Garden (Chapter Seven), don't fake it till you make it. Live it and it will lead you to where you are meant to be.

When you get so attached to the image of what you should be, you'll end up looking to the world around you to define you. Because *should* doesn't come from you. It comes from your surroundings. When you are born into this world, you are yourself. Authentically. As you grow, your surroundings tell you what's right and wrong. Who you should and shouldn't be.

And, sometimes, after you embody that image of who you should be, you feel a sense of responsibility to keep up with it, to keep performing it perfectly. I see this happening quite often with moms, for example. Women are often conditioned to believe that motherhood is the mark of womanhood . . . that it's the most important achievement a woman could ever accomplish. While it's okay to believe that, it's also okay not to. Not every woman can bear children, and not every woman wants to. The point here is this: If you follow that path because society has convinced you to, then you have the underlying belief that once you reach that destination, you will be enough. You will be okay.

It's the same with any other goal, path, or label you are currently convincing yourself you need in order to "make it." In order to be enough. And once you're there, you try so hard to show the world that you can handle it . . . that not only are you surviving, you are thriving. You start getting your validation from the world's approval of how well you fit the mold. But if you took a second to look in the mirror and asked yourself *Is this what I really want?* the truth would reveal itself to you.

When you work so hard to conform to outside expectations, you abandon yourself. You abandon who you really are.

So when you look at yourself in the mirror, literally or meta-phorically, your focus is probably on the blur. All you can see is who you *should* be, what more you need to do to be welcomed. You speak to yourself with the words others have said to you.

And all those things further cloud your vision and stop you from truly seeing yourself. It's like looking into a mirror that hasn't been cleaned in decades—you're lucky if you see your shadow in it.

Over the years, that's what I noticed about myself. To take you on my journey of cleaning the mirror, I will tell you some stories. Let's start with an excerpt from a poem I read for the first time at a diversity event in 2016.

Pillar #1: Know the Story of You

WHAT STORY DO I TELL YOU?

> *If I were to tell you my story,*
> *I'd wonder:*
> *What story do I tell you?*
> *Do I tell you the story of the little girl*
> *who was bullied in school?*
> *The story of the girl*
> *who was always told she was too sensitive?*
> *Do I tell you the story of the girl who*
> *lived in 2, 3, 4, 5, 6, 7 I can't remember*
> *how many homes?*
> *Or do I tell you the story of the girl*
> *who never felt that she had a voice?*
> *Always quiet.*

Always "okay."
Never the one to be asked
"How was your day?"
Never the one told
"I love you."
Do I tell you the story of the girl who
moved to a new country on her sixteenth birthday?
Who saw flames in the airport she was in a few weeks back
on TV?
Do I tell you the story of the girl who
almost lost her father when she was twelve years old?
Do I tell you the story of the girl
who never felt that she had a home?
The one who spent her life building homes
in other people
begging to be welcomed?
To feel loved?
To feel valued?
To feel respected?
Which story do I tell you
when the only story that you might see
when you see me
is this (pointing to my hijab)?
it's as if what I have wrapped around my head
is wrapped around all of the stories that
I lived.
It's as if what's wrapped around my head
not only covers my hair
but covers the human me.

Covers that little girl I just told you about.
Covers the woman I am today.
I live in a place and in a time when
people want to condense me into
this.
They forget about the world within me.
The wonder within me.
The depth within me.
They forget about the voice that's aching to roar
from within me
as if what's wrapped around my head is
wrapped around my mouth.
So, which story do I tell you?
Do I tell you the story of the girl on the bus
who was told not to dress like that
because she's in Canada?
Or the story of the girl who
is always looked at as oppressed?
The girl who's always asked,
why do you wear that?
in a way that makes me feel I am incomplete
because I choose to cover my head.
In a way that makes me feel that something about me
is fundamentally wrong because
there are parts of my body that I choose not to show.
And it saddens me that many people believe
that this *is the worst thing that could have happened to me.*
And it makes them not see
all of the other stories buried within me,

as if my stories are written on my skin
and hidden by the clothes that I dress my body with.
I am so afraid to break in front of anyone
because part of me is afraid that they will not see
that I'm heartbroken, because of the world, not because of
    this.
That I'm voiceless, because of the world, not because of
    this.
That I'm hurt by the world, not by this.
And they just might tell me
that I am broken,
voiceless
and hurt BECAUSE of this.
That is the side of me that you see
but when I come home every day,
and this *comes off,*
oh how I wish that all of my troubles
were gone too.
Oh how I wish that things were this simple.
That if I took this *off,*
I all of a sudden would be heard
or that my heart's pieces that feel too broken
would be sewn back together.
or that the chains that hold the voice inside of me captive
would just disappear
and that my voice would roar.

I read this poem at multiple events to address the importance of looking beneath a person's surface. Beneath the labels. At the time, I still wore my hijab, the traditional headdress worn by many women who embrace the Muslim faith. It's worthy to note that not all Muslim women wear it, and that there are different beliefs among those who identify with the faith on the obligatory aspect of it.

At the time I wrote this poem, I had already self-published my first two books, *Mind Platter* and *The Nectar of Pain*. I was well aware that what the world celebrated about me was my resilience and strength as a visibly Muslim woman who writes well. Even though my writing had absolutely nothing to do with religion or culture, multiple news articles and reviews referred to me as an immigrant Muslim woman who wrote about her journey from Lebanon to Canada, which was not even close to reality. My parents got married in Canada, had five children, decided to move to Lebanon, and that's where I was born. I was a Canadian citizen weeks after I was born, and I'd visited my family in Canada multiple times. My older siblings made their way back to Canada one after the other while I stayed with my dad and multiple relatives in Lebanon until my sixteenth birthday. At that point, every member of my family, except for my married sister, was in Canada. I came to visit, and shortly after, the war broke out in Lebanon, so I stayed in Canada. The point is not to run away from labels. The point is to say *That is not my story. You don't get to take what I look like and use that to tell the story you think it means about me. I tell my story.* Was I an immigrant? Absolutely. Everywhere I went. Even when I lived in Lebanon. Because I never felt the true feeling of *home*. Was I Muslim? Yes. But why did that have to be part of my title? Why did that have to be more important than what I was actually doing?

When I wrote this poem, I was trying so hard to show everyone around me that I was experiencing pain. The pain of not being seen—really seen. I was hiding years of searching for home. I was hiding how out of place I felt. I was hiding how humiliated and emotionally debilitated I was to have experienced sexual harassment and power abuse. As I read this poem, I was standing on stage, screaming without screaming: HEAR ME. See me. Believe me. See past my labels. See past what you see with your eyes. Let your heart see me.

I would always get asked to speak at events and in classrooms, and the topic always somehow ended up being religion, culture, or the hijab. And I wanted to say *There is more to me.*

I was changing. My beliefs were changing.

And I was more than a Muslim woman who wore the hijab and happened to have the ability to write.

I was no longer the sixteen-year-old sheltered girl who came to Canada with all the beliefs taught to me in my tiny village back in Lebanon.

Remember how at the beginning of this chapter I said that not seeing yourself clearly is more detrimental than the world's not seeing you? That's exactly what I was doing here. I was asking to be seen and heard without my actually seeing myself. I was asking the world around me to lift the layers—the shame and the fear—that stood in the way of me being myself instead of just doing it myself and not caring what the world thought. I was asking for permission to tell the stories that, as I wrote in the poem, were written on my skin, hidden under the clothes I wore.

I was waiting for someone to unveil me. To save me. But the hardest, yet most liberating truth, was that I needed to unveil myself. I could easily hide behind my words and hope that someone out there would understand me. But I knew I couldn't hide anymore.

So the process of unveiling began.

I don't remember the exact moment it began. In a way, I had been unveiling within myself for a while. But remember that one night when my dad told me I'd lost the look I once had in my eyes? That was a major moment of realizing how far I'd traveled from myself. That was the beginning of something exploding inside of me. This ache to return to myself, even though I didn't know what "myself" was or what I was returning to. In retrospect, it was home that I was returning to . . . *me* that I was returning to.

In my TEDx speech on finding home through poetry, I describe seeing myself that night like this: "I remember that night looking in the mirror at a person I didn't recognize. I had no idea who she was. My face didn't resemble me. My features actually looked distorted. I felt like I was looking at a sky when it was just choking on grayness—no sun, no clouds, no rain, nothing, just choking."

Pillar #2: Unveil and Deconstruct the You the World Told You to Be—Be Who You Are

To unveil, I had to start by asking myself how I came to be . . . in order to unravel that and re-create a *me* I could recognize in the mirror. I started asking questions. I became curious. I took an inventory of what my current life was like and asked myself the following question about each part of it: *If I had a choice, is this what I would choose?*

Would I choose to keep quiet about my experience of power abuse and sexual harassment? No. But I can't share it, because no one would understand. No one would believe me. Was it really that bad, or am I just exaggerating? Plus my reputation would be ruined because I was emotionally involved with a man, period.

Would I choose to keep waiting for the moment when a man comes and proposes so I can get married and start a family and fulfill my destiny as a woman? No. But that's how it should be, right?

Would I choose to live at home? No. But I can't move out because culturally and religiously, it's frowned upon. I'm not married yet.

Would I choose to wear the hijab? No. But I can't take it off now, because I've been wearing it for so long and everyone will think I'm condemning it . . . that I want to show my body, which is so shameful to want to do. They will think I'm asking for attention. Plus it would ruin the image of the good girl I've been building for so long.

To BEGIN THE UNVEILING of your authentic self, let's start by assessing your life in the Blank Canvas mirror.

The Blank Canvas Mirror

Imagine this mirror as a canvas of your life.

1. On a whiteboard or paper, write down exactly what your life looks like now (take an inventory of your life).

2. Ask yourself: Does this canvas actually reflect *me*?

    a. Ask yourself: If I had a choice, is this what I would choose?

    b. Put a check mark where you say yes and an X where you say no.

3. Start a new board or piece of paper. Imagine the canvas of your life blank.

4. If this canvas actually reflected **you** and all your choices, what would it look like?

5. Ask yourself: What changes do I need to make to go from my current life to the life I choose?

That's what I did.

And I knew living the life that actually reflected me would require courage. I'd have to unveil the self underneath all those layers to expose my authentic self. But my authentic self would find it very easy to say no to the life I *thought* I should be living and yes to the life I *want* to be living.

So, after reporting my story privately and not feeling heard, I shared it publicly. And I braved through what was said about me. I learned that *reputation* is just a word invented to keep us women living in shame. I learned it's not my responsibility to be the torchbearer for my culture and religion. I learned I can live with my reputation being ruined. Because from that ruin, I discovered that my worth is not built on or broken down by ideals placed by society, culture, or religion. My worth is built on me. It's built within me.

A reporter called me at the time and said: "When I first met you, you were like a loose leaf in the wind. And I look at you now and think . . . wow! You know what you stand for."

It's the strength I gained from standing up for myself that gave me the push to express that I no longer fear men. I no longer fear men with power. I no longer fear being a woman. I no longer feel incomplete unless I get married. I remember once sitting in a gathering of women where one woman said of her cousin, "She's almost twenty-two. Of course she's going to worry about not being married yet." I looked over and said "Worried? I'm twenty-seven."

It's the strength I gained from being able to speak words like that, to call out hypocrisy when I see it, that gave me the push to say I wanted to move out of my parents' home. Was it easy? Of course not. Even though I was twenty-seven years old, I felt so ashamed of saying I wanted to live on my own. Because I was going against the rules. And why would I want to live alone? What could I possibly want to do when no one is watching? But I did it. I found a place. And I moved out.

It's the strength I gained from being able to make that move that pushed me to say "I want to take my hijab off." If I could go back to the moment when I decided to wear it in seventh grade and ask myself if I wanted to wear it, I would have said no.

Do you see how my unveiling was not just about the physical unveiling? It was a process of deconstructing everything I'd learned was right and wrong and asking myself: Do you believe that's right or wrong? What do *you* think about this?

I unveiled the story.

I unveiled my wants and needs.

I unveiled my voice.

I unveiled my hair and my body.

I unveiled myself.

I wrote this chapter from scratch at least five times, because I was struggling with pinpointing that one big magical moment when it all turned around . . . when the unveiling happened. As you can see, there was no one big moment. This wasn't a Hollywood movie. There were many little big moments that had to happen. There were moments that built up resilience for other moments to happen.

୧

What would your life look like if you lived it as you wanted
to, not as you were convinced you needed to live it?

୧

Pillar #3: Don't Let Guilt Stop You— Let It Teach You

When you're trying to remove the blur that's standing between you
and the mirror, you most definitely will experience guilt. You will
feel you've done something wrong. It's such an uncomfortable emotion that you might want to keep the blur in the mirror rather than
deal with it. But remember that guilt is a normal emotion to experience when you're going against what you've believed for so long.

୧

Unveiling your authentic self may take a while. It may feel
untrue to yourself to be going against how you've always
been. This doesn't mean you're on the wrong path. It just
means you are changing. Just like unveiling, clearing a
mirror that hasn't been cleared in ages may take a while.
And the image you see in it may take a while to get used
to. You might feel foreign to yourself . . . foreign to the
self you've been for so long. But wasn't that the self that
was constantly building homes in others, waiting to be
welcomed? Your unveiled self is the ultimate at-home self.

୧

When I decided to take my hijab off, I cannot even begin to explain to you how guilty I felt for wanting to show my hair and my body. The first time I walked outside with some of my hair and my neck showing, I felt naked. I felt so guilty for wanting that. I felt guilty for enjoying the wind blowing through my hair, the sun touching my skin. I felt like I needed to explain to everyone why I wanted to take my hijab off. It was only with time that I understood that what I do with my body is no one's business but mine.

I started wearing the hijab when I was attending the Islamic school in Lebanon. I was in seventh grade and would have been twelve years old at that point. I wanted to look like my older sister. And I wanted to be the best "good girl" I could be. Wearing the hijab meant that I took one step closer to God. There was this hidden, but felt, judgment toward girls who didn't wear it.

At that school, we were taught that the hijab was mandatory and that we couldn't enter heaven without having worn it on this earth, in this life. One teacher went as far as telling us that girls who didn't wear it would be hung by their hair in the afterlife. This has no basis in the Quran itself, but it was part of the ancient man-made tactics of scaring women into conforming to the rules.

I didn't wear the hijab out of fear. I wore it because I wanted to be a good girl. I wanted to be closer to God. Most women around me wore it, so I didn't stand out in any way. It felt more like I fit in.

I remember the day when I decided to wear it, my dad asked to speak with me at the end of the day.

"Did someone tell you you have to wear it? You don't have to if you don't want to."

"I want to wear it."

"Are you sure?" he asked again. "I don't want you to think I want you to wear it. It's a personal choice. It's up to you."

I felt like such a grown-up, being able to say *This is what I want.*

I won't lie. There were times after that when, shortly after I'd bathe, I'd look at my hair and wish I could go out in the sun with it showing. I loved my hair. I loved how the brown in it turned to gold in the sun. But now that I'd decided to cover it, I had to stick to that choice. And the struggle itself in keeping it on, or following any re-ligious rules, meant that we were on the right path. Because we were taught that the "right" path was hard to stick to. We were taught that that was the true meaning of *jihad:* the struggle of the soul to stay spiritually close to God by following the rules and avoiding any sinful behavior.

As I mentioned earlier, and as I referenced in "What Story Do I Tell You?,"when I moved to Canada at age sixteeen, my family was already here. I'd visited Canada many times before, but only for the summer. My dad took me aside one night, as he had years earlier, and said, "You're going to be *living* in a new country now and people here are different. I know that you are sensitive and I want to make sure you know that if you want to take your hijab off, that's okay."

The hijab had become part of my identity and how I saw myself. It was like a safety blanket that I wasn't ready to let go of. It was how I'd seen myself for a few years now. It represented the image of the good, faithful girl I was convinced I needed to be. So I kept it on. I wasn't aware that I was seen differently until the story I'm about to share with you. This story was pivotal in my journey with the hijab.

I am on the bus, on my way to university. I am wearing a long jean skirt that my sister gave me and a white shirt with little pink and blue flowers on it. I am wearing my favorite white hijab. I make my way to the back of the bus, and that's when I see an older man staring me down. I don't think much of it.

For a good ten minutes, he's looking at me with what I can only describe as intensity. His body is covered in tattoos. That's all I can focus on. He gets up to get off at his stop, stands at the door as it opens, looks back at me and says, "You know you're in Canada. You don't have to dress like that." Then he jumps off the bus.

I put my head down. Tears start streaming down my face. The woman in front of me turns around and says: "I am so sorry. That was not okay. You can dress however you want."

The rest is a blur.

I am now fully aware that I stand out. I am fully aware that maybe being *Canadian* doesn't include me . . . maybe it doesn't include the way I look. Maybe it doesn't include my safety blanket.

The next morning, as I get ready for school, I look in the mirror. I grab my hijab before I wrap it around my head and I ask myself *Who am I? What do I stand for?*

Why am I wearing this? Is it important? Is it worth it? Why don't I just take it off and not put up with this kind of judgment? Does everyone see me this way? Is that why I was treated badly in the first job I had? Is that why I feel so isolated and out of place?

The questions swirling in my mind are endless. They hurt.

I tell myself: *If not wearing this means you will please the eyes of others, then taking it off is weakness. Waking up every morning and saying "I choose to wear this"—that's strength. That's courage.*

Who am I? I am the courageous one.

What do I stand for? Courage.

So, that day, I chose courage. And on the day that I walked out of my apartment for the first time with a strand of hair and my neck showing, I remembered the questions I'd asked myself:

Who am I? I am the courageous one.

What do I stand for? Courage.

So, that day, I chose courage, too. I faced criticism, yes. I lost probably a couple hundred thousand followers on social media over time because of that decision. At the same time, so many ran to congratulate me on being "free." And all I wanted to say was *I am not free because I took my hijab off. I am free because I made that choice.* The day I chose to continue to wear it after my incident on the bus at nineteen, I was free. And the day I chose to take it off, at twenty-eight, I was free. I didn't want anyone to define for me what liberation was. And I say to you: *Don't let anyone define liberation for you.*

But to get to this point, I needed to understand where my guilt stemmed from. And that was from my school education in my younger years, which taught me I couldn't be a good, pious girl without wearing it.

Pillar #4: Use Confusion as a Road to Clarity

My biggest moments of confusion led me to the best decisions of my life in terms of doing what honors building a home within myself. Being unable to decipher people's behavior—one day welcoming me into their lives and the next day making me feel like a stranger—led me to feel confused. Because, let's be honest, confusing behavior in others makes you question yourself. You question your own sanity, your own recollection of events . . . your own understanding of the events . . . of the person . . . of yourself . . .

As painful as it may be, confusion will put you eye to eye with all the changes you need to make in order to never put clarity in someone else's hands. Inside of someone else's home.

Let me show you. I want to take you on a journey I call *Delusion*.

Part 1: Imagine coming home at the end of a long day. You park your car. You walk up to the door. And take out your keys. You try to open the door, but the key won't turn. The door won't open. At first, you look around to see if you're in the right place. You're in disbelief because you've been coming home to this house every single day. So you start questioning yourself. Did I take the wrong road? Did I park in the wrong place? You start knocking but no one opens. You know deep in your heart that this is the place you come home to every single day. Imagine how shattering that can be. You won't know where to go. Or what to do. And because it's the home you've always come to, you come back every day. But the key still doesn't work. One day, the person who lives there finally opens the door. You smile in relief and attempt to walk inside, but they look at you as if they have no idea who you are. You recognize them but they look at you as if they've never seen you before. In fact, they tell you to stop trying to open the door or they will call the police. So in the middle of your denial, disbelief, and confusion, you have to walk away. Otherwise, you will be in trouble. And it's not like you have time to be in pain or to make sense of what just

happened . . . You just know that the reality you once thought
you had is no longer there.

Now, imagine that story, but instead of a physical home,
replace it with a human who was there for you long enough to
feel like home. A person who laid the foundation of a home.
Imagine coming home to that person, to that soul space that you
once shared, to find that that person is no longer open to you.
And instead of the key, you try all the things you tried before.
You try being kind and loving, being your old self. But nothing
works. They look at you as if they have no idea who you are.

And it just doesn't make sense that someone who knew you,
the real you, no longer recognizes you. What's the first thing
you do? You start questioning yourself, especially if you two
were the only ones who knew of that home. The whole existence
of that home is in your hands. It depends on whether you see it
or not. So you start knocking on that door, on the heart of that
person. And there's no answer. In fact, you're told to stay away
and when you ask why, you're told that there is no place for
you. And when you ask why all of a sudden there's no place
for you, you're told that there never was a place for you and
you're delusional for believing that. There you are, left in the
middle of a road you started walking without knowing where
it was leading. You started walking with one person who you
trusted deeply to get you to the right place. You've lost sight
of where you started, because your focus was not on the road
but on who you were walking it with. And now that person has
vanished and has convinced you they were never there. And it's
not like you have time to grieve, because the whole experience
disappeared and you were told it never happened.

If you think about it, something must be wrong with you,
they tell you. So the trauma from that moment lives inside of
you, but you're not allowed to feel it. You're not allowed to
heal from it, because you're told you made it up. It's like try-
ing to heal from a disease without having anyone validate the
diagnosis.

I wrote this to describe experiencing the shock of abandonment. I receive the same story in different iterations daily. Take Sally, who found out her husband had been cheating on her their entire sixteen years of marriage. They had two children together. When she reached out to me to tell me that, she told me the worst part of it all was how he would tell her she was insecure every time she questioned his absences or the behavior that made her question his loyalty to her. How he would tell her she was crazy to ever think that he was having an affair with someone else. Even though she saw him hide his phone all the time. Even though she had every reason to believe something wasn't right. She believed she was crazy and was overreacting by believing her own gut.

Take Sena, who moved to Canada from Pakistan after she got married. She told me, "I did not know the extent of the damage of his gaslighting. I disappeared. I went from being super confident to constantly questioning my existence. He made me go on antidepressants at the beginning of our relationship, and I went numb. Over the years, it felt like my being was being chipped away by control and belittling. I didn't realize how destroyed I was until I heard you explain the word *gaslighting*. I had no idea there was such a thing. I accepted that something was wrong with me. I'm still having a hard time detaching from what destroyed me."

I define *gaslighting* as the denial of your reality by someone you trust—whatever reality it is you experience with them. I bring it up in this chapter because it is the ultimate, albeit extreme, form of confusion. It often happens in relationships, but it also happens in politics, the workplace, friendships, and family relationships. It can cause damage that seems irreversible. The term comes from the 1938 British play *Gas Light,* in which an abusive husband manipulates his wife into believing that she's crazy by psychologically destroying her perception of reality. One of his tactics was to manipulate the level of the gas light in their home so it keeps dimming and then returning to normal. It frightens her, but when she comments on it, he claims she's mistaken, making her think she's losing her mind.

I was called delusional by a man multiple times when I reminded him of things he said. He would tell me that I was making it all up in my head. And even though I had text messages to prove it to myself, I still questioned my recollection of events, because I trusted him. My trust in him overrode my trust in myself. That doesn't even scratch the surface, but I tell only parts of the story, being cautious not to throw myself back into the darkness of it.

The day that I discovered the word *gaslighting,* I felt like my confusion, my blurry vision, was magically starting to clear. Because now I could start making sense of what happened.

Labeling the experience allows you to know you are not alone. And it also clears your vision. It validates you. Receiving the validation that your experience actually has a name and that others have gone, and continue to go, through it . . . there is something relieving about that.

*Once you are able to label your experience,
you have already experienced clarity.*

Remember when Sena said, "I didn't realize how destroyed I was until you explained the word *gaslighting*?" She sent that message to me in a voice note. The relief I heard in her voice was unreal. Because when she heard a word that embodied her story, she felt internally validated. Once that happens, you can separate yourself from the experience.

*You are not confused. You are experiencing a confusing
situation. Separate the confusing situation from who
you are. If you say "I am confused," you are implying
the confusing situation is part of you. It is not. It is part
of what you are experiencing. The answer to the confusion
does not lie in the confusion itself. Rather it lies in the
ability to step outside of it and see that you are experiencing
it instead of it being you. The answer lies in you.*

Pillar #5: Listen to Your Gut (Your Instincts)

If something doesn't feel right in a way you can't explain, it probably isn't right. It's your body telling you something is off.

But don't we sometimes run away from what's good for us? Yes. It could very well be that something good is coming your way, but you don't *feel* good about it, because it's unfamiliar. I will address this more in the Surrender room, but for the purposes of the Clarity room, I want you to listen to your gut. Whether or not you go with it isn't the issue. This is about not ignoring that it's trying to tell you something. To know what it's trying to tell you, you'll need to go inward.

Throughout my situationship with Noah, I always felt something was wrong. I just didn't listen to my gut. I hoped it was wrong. I mistook the highs and lows of the confusion for liking him. Amir Levine and Rachel Heller (authors of *Attached*) refer to this as an activated attachment system. Because I hadn't built that home within myself and didn't have the security of truly internalizing my worthiness of love, I took his unavailability as a cue to work harder to prove my worth. His emotional unavailability confirmed my *Why can't I have that?* story. It activated the anxious attachment style I'd developed in my childhood and put me back into the body of that little girl who was aching to get what she didn't have. He always had his guard up. He always showed a little bit of himself, just enough to keep me from letting go.

But here is where the manipulation came in. Here is where my gut was saying RUN. But I didn't listen to it. I actually ignored it. In moments when he'd sense that I was letting him go, he'd tell me something self-denigrating like "I've never felt confident because of my upbringing," knowing that I'd jump into savior mode and fight his demons for him. I'm an empath, remember? I'm not saying this to blame him for my actions. I take full responsibility for trying to lift him up. No one can force you to do anything, after all. But when it comes to emotional investment, logic isn't exactly the first instinct to kick in.

He would lead me to a point where he'd say, "Be vulnerable. Tell me how you feel about me." And as soon as I did, he would be so happy. But he would never reciprocate. And as soon as I asked for something as simple as meeting up for coffee, he would immediately turn into someone I didn't recognize. He would say, "I'm not ready for anything serious." And I'd immediately jump into defense mode and say, "I'm sorry. I didn't mean that. I just feel like it's a natural next step in whatever this is." I was so confused. I had no idea what he wanted. I had no idea why he continued to seek moments of connection with me that truly resembled a relationship when he was going to eventually shoot me down.

And the funny part is, every single one of my friends not only hated him . . . they despised him. They didn't see what I saw in him. You see, I fabricated this image of a wounded man who needed someone to believe in him and be patient with him when his actions resembled those of a boy with the emotional maturity of a twelve-year-old.

Had I listened to my gut, which was telling me *This is not right. This doesn't feel right or healthy at all*, I would have saved myself so much grief.

Even though I hate admitting it, I also experienced gaslighting with Noah. But I didn't know it or realize it until I'd distanced myself from the experience long enough to see it clearly. One simple example was the following: The first time that Noah asked me to go for coffee, he'd asked me to tell him when coffee would work. So I told him my schedule. We met. Halfway through coffee, he asked me, "So why did you want to meet for coffee?" All I was thinking was *You're the one who asked me to go for coffee!* That should have been my first indication that he wanted me to believe that I was chasing after him.

But I didn't listen to my gut.

That night, I drove to my friend Jenan's place after having coffee with Noah. To this day, she tells me that she hates him because of how gray I looked that night. She tells me that she knew something was wrong.

Pillar #6: See the Story as It Is, Not as You Want It to Be, Not as You Wish It Were

When you are feeling confusion, your soul is searching for clarity. And clarity cannot be seen when it's clouded by your wishes or your delusions about what the truth is. Just as you can't see yourself clearly in the mirror when you cloud your vision with what you thought you should be, it's the same situation with other experiences in your life. The truth is often right in front of you. It's right within you. And full acceptance of it is often blocked by denial.

When you choose denial and confusion, what does that indicate? You probably guessed it . . . You're searching for home, for clarity, inside of someone else. On a foundation other than your own.

There was a part of me that fell into complete denial that I could have been gaslighted by someone, especially Noah. How could I, after everything I'd been through, be gaslighted? Noah was the one I was saving. He was the one I was lifting. How could Noah, the broken little boy on the inside, be capable of creating this much conflict and confusion inside of me? It can't be.

But it is.

It is.

I had to accept that.

And I didn't accept that until I stopped looking for clarity inside of him. Until I stopped trying to make sense of him. I had to look for clarity inside of myself. I had to look at what it was inside of me that made me hold on to the brokenness inside of someone else . . . that made me assume responsibility for fixing the damage he had in his life. And I had to stop trying to prepare him to be the person I needed.

You need to stop seeing others as you wanted them to be, or as you thought they were. You need to see them as they actually are. You need to stop seeing the story as your in-denial-self wants to see it.

You have to stop seeing that person as they were when you first developed feelings for them. I know that sounds easier said than done. I know that some events and feelings are irreversible. So don't reverse them. Honor them. But also honor that they're no longer here. Honor that there are new events and new feelings that need to be honored as well. You can't keep looking back to the version you saw before the events that caused you to see someone's true self. For example, when you discover that someone's been lying to you for your entire relationship, you can't continue to see them as you saw them before you discovered the lies. Well, you can, but why choose to? It's like continuing to believe the earth is flat when you know it's actually round.

Let's go back to *Delusion*.

> *Part 2: You need to focus on putting your broken pieces back together and when you do, you'll be able to stitch them together with gold to make a new version of yourself.*

Don't resent your sincerity and empathy or believe they were the reason you were taken advantage of. Understand it's not what's inside of you that allows others to take advantage of you. It's what they choose to do with what they see in you. And it's not what others do with what they see in you that makes you who you are. It's what's within you that makes you who you are.

It's not anyone else's home you need to be welcomed into. It's your own home you need to be welcomed into.

Stop searching for someone to lead you to the end of the road, because you will lose yourself looking for someone else. And you have to stop looking for the delusion of the person you once saw. You have to start focusing on the road. And when you do, you will pave your own road. Yes, it might be dark, and you might not know where you're headed. But as long as you are moving toward yourself, you will reach home.

You will reach home.

Pillar #7: Stop Looking for a Speck of Dust in the Ocean

When we're looking for clarity, especially in relationships, we can easily get lost in looking for something that's just not there. In cases like this, you need to take a step back, distance yourself from the situation, and see the bigger picture. If you get too close to the mirror, you get so focused on details that minor things start to exaggerate themselves in your eyes. That's the power of your attention. Take a step back from the mirror and try to see the story as a whole.

When your mind endlessly cycles over every detail, wondering what could have gone wrong or how someone could be so cruel toward you or how someone could see ugliness in you, and when you get frustrated with yourself for not being able to stop thinking about it, here is what I want you to remember.

Sometimes people will do things that hurt you without thinking of the kind of pain that they're causing you. And it doesn't necessarily make them bad people. That's not up to you to decide. The truth is, getting stuck in being angry or upset with someone over them hurting you doesn't bring you any peace at all. It's only going to bring you more pain.

What you're looking for is closure. And your hope is that once you understand why they did what they did, you'll be able to move on. But . . . spending all that time going over every single detail and hoping that, somehow, within the folds of those details you're going to find your answer is like looking for a speck of dust in an ocean. You're never going to find it. Because that's not what you need to be focused on. What you need to focus on is that the person who hurt you doesn't deserve your time or your energy more than you do. That person might not even deserve it at all. You are the one who deserves that time and energy. And even though it hurts so much, cry it out, talk it out, write it out, dance it out, scream it out. Do whatever you need to do for it to leave. Don't you ever look for the cure in the poison. It's just not there. The cure is inside of you. If you are hurt because you gave love, kindness, and understanding, then come to yourself for that love, kindness, and understanding.

Let them keep what they took from you. That's how you spread your light in the world. Don't fight to take it back. Fighting to understand and get justification or closure is fighting to get back what you gave. Just let them take it. Even if what you got in return was pain, poison, rude words, and arrows aimed at your heart, self-esteem, and self-worth. Let them take it.

That's what they're able to give. And maybe they're able to give more, but they're choosing to give you what they're giving you now. And if they were able to give more, why would you want someone in your life who's going to actively choose to hurt you? You don't want that.

It hurts because they meant something to you. It hurts because you believed them. It hurts because you saw a future with them. Because you were vulnerable with them, because you spent so much of your time and energy on them. Of course that's going to hurt. So it's okay for it to hurt. Let it. Sit with the pain. This should never be your normal. You should never be okay with being treated badly. You should never be okay with being betrayed. You should never be okay with having someone you trusted so much turn around and treat you as if you never meant anything to them. You should never be okay with that.

You don't have to be okay with it to accept it. And you have to accept it because healing comes with accepting it. The empathy, sensitivity, and beauty that allows you to feel the pain of being treated that way makes you who you are. It's why you're able to give love. It's why you're able to give, period. You choose not to cause pain. And that's what makes you who you are.

So stop looking for the reason someone hurt you. Stop looking for why they changed. Stop looking for that speck of dust in the ocean and look at the ocean as a whole. If you're able to just let that closure, that person, that experience dissolve altogether in the big ocean of your life and all the people you're going to meet and all the love you're going to experience, give, and receive . . . if you're able to do that, then you'll see how small that person and that experience are compared to the glory of what you can experience. But when you're looking for something that's not there, you're just going to drown. You're just going to suffocate if you truly believe that there's no way for you to get out unless you find that speck of dust. So let it dissolve. Let it go away. And keep swimming. Keep living. Keep breathing. Keep moving toward the places and the people who don't demand that you swallow yourself, that you drown within yourself, for them to see you.

Pillar #8: Don't Cloud Your Vision by Curbing Anger

How many times have you convinced yourself that all you need to do is *calm down?* That expressing anger is somehow a sign of weakness? How many times have you said "It's okay" in response to an apology when it really wasn't okay? When you knew that the apology itself couldn't take away the pain you felt?

Understand that not allowing yourself to be angry doesn't make you a good or a calm person. Not allowing yourself to be angry will stop you from seeing the story as it is. It will stop you from seeing yourself as you are. It will block your vision from seeing the truth. From seeing *your* truth. What we were never taught is that anger is a healthy and normal human emotion that is meant to bring us relief and resolution. It's meant to be an alarm that says *Be careful! Something here is threatening!* And when we stop ourselves from expressing it (even worse, stop ourselves from feeling it), it could be—actually, it definitely will be—detrimental to our clarity.

Feeling anger doesn't mean there's something wrong with you. And by the same token, the fact that there's something happening to you that makes you angry doesn't mean there's something wrong with you.

∽

Instead of punishing yourself for feeling angry,
ask yourself What is this anger trying to tell me?
Is it trying to tell me that my boundaries are being violated?
Is it trying to tell me that I'm being silenced?
Is it trying to tell me that I should actually say no?

∽

Especially when it comes to women, we are taught to stay quiet. We are taught that anger isn't feminine—that it's a turnoff. We're taught to apologize for expressing our feelings in ways that come off as aggressive when we're really just expressing our boundaries or that a boundary has been crossed. But if a man spoke with anger, it would be considered completely normal, even manly.

Think of anger as a fire ignited inside you. The wood is our boundaries, beliefs, self-respect, our voice. The matches are triggers (either external, through the actions of others, or internal, through our own internalization of what other people's behaviors must mean about us). Air is its power. And anger burns and grows just as fire does. Keeping it inside will only burn you. Fully putting it outside, projecting it onto others, will burn someone else, which sometimes is needed.

For example, when you say no to someone, you may be burning them with that fire. And that's okay. Because you are not curbing your own desires just to please someone.

You want to learn how to manage the fire of anger, not suppress it at the cost of what you really want to say. Suppressing it is the same as giving it more power, more air, to keep burning.

I often get told "I just can't see you being angry." The younger, sheltered, naïve girl I was would say, "I never get angry. I have healthy ways of calming my feelings of anger." Now I say, "Just because I don't scream, it doesn't mean I'm not angry."

Anger sounds like *no*.

Anger sounds like *That's not right.*

Anger sounds like *This is making me uncomfortable. Stop it.*

Anger sounds like *You can't do that.*

Anger sounds like standing on stage when I was being legally threatened for sharing my story publicly—in front of people I was warned would be watching me—and saying *I will not apologize for telling my truth. I will not apologize for raising my voice.*

Let me take you to the day of my speech.

I see so many faces of people who I recognize. My lawyer is

sitting next to me. I know that they will be angry with what I have to say. I start breathing heavily, knowing that everything that I will say will be used against me.

But then I remember.

I remember the girl who walked outside of that office feeling like a girl with broken wings. I remember the girl who was so terrified the night before she reported that she collapsed on the kitchen floor and screamed to her mother for help. I remember the look in my mom's eyes as she desperately, on the verge of tears, said, "Something is going on with you and you're not telling us." I remember the girl sitting in the investigator's office, who started hyperventilating as soon as he told her the lies the witnesses had told.

I remember her.

And I become angry.

The fire within me starts to rage, and as I'm walking on stage, I feel wings of fire surrounding me. I take with me every moment of anger. And I stand. Tall. And proud.

My voice trembles as I begin to read, but the more I speak, the more courage I have. And this takes me back to what I said earlier about how there isn't one moment that completely changes your life. There are a series of moments that feed each other. It's like a domino effect.

I speak for twenty minutes, during which I look to the audience, not knowing who exactly is watching. But I know there are enough people there in positions of power who have the ability to effect injustice just as they do justice. And I want them to listen. I can see tears in many people's eyes, especially women. And I know it's because they know; they've experienced what I experienced.

I end my speech by raising the stack of papers I was served and saying *I will not apologize for telling my truth.*

I then read a poem by Jasmin Kaur:

> *Scream*
> *so that one day*
> *a hundred years from now*
> *another sister will not have to*
> *dry her tears wondering*
> *where in history*
> *she lost her voice.*

Then I said: I screamed, as loud as I possibly can. Will you scream with me?

I ask you the same question. Will you scream with me?

Will you scream for yourself?

> *Your anger doesn't have to*
> *look like anger.*
> *Your anger doesn't have to*
> *sound like anger.*
> *Your anger can be the softest,*
> *kindest,*
> *gentlest*
> *whisper that says*
> no
> *and sends echoes in the world*
> *on the wings of the butterfly*
> *they told you would never*

leave her cocoon.
Your no *doesn't have to*
sound like no.
Your no *doesn't have to*
look like no.
Your no *can be turning the*
fire that they tried to burn you with,
that they tried to turn you to ashes with,
into a match
that ignites a flame
that gives rise to the phoenix
they told you
would never rise.

Additional Mirrors in This Room

THE PURPOSE MIRROR

Look in this mirror to understand your purpose, your "why." This could be related to any work or action that you are doing.

The following questions will help you evaluate what you're currently doing and whether it aligns with your purpose. Your purpose could be a job or any form of occupation in life.

1. What am I doing now? (actions)

2. What is my end goal in doing this? (purpose)

3. Do my actions align with that purpose?

   a. If yes, great!

   b. If not, what do I need to change?

These questions might seem too simple, but when you take time to answer them, you'll see clearly how they will push you to reflect, redirect your actions, or reassure yourself that you're on the right track.

There was a short period of time when I found myself focusing too much on social media metrics. Brands usually ask for impressions, reach, demographics, and the like. Most of the circle of professionals I surrounded myself with defined themselves by their number of views and followers. At the time, I didn't have daily check-ins with myself, and my focus on metrics ended up impacting me. It's easy to get caught up in evaluating your success with numbers when it's obvious that the world evaluates you the same way. But at the end of the day, you don't want to be seeing yourself the way that the world sees you, or change yourself to what the world values so you can feel that value. You want to be true to yourself so you can see and feel your real value and then project it into the world. I felt completely thrown off by metrics and asked my team to make a plan for the number of posts we needed to pump out per day, at what times, and so forth. But that felt so . . . not right. I felt like a hypocrite. I got caught up in what everyone else was doing on social media, so I stopped trusting myself.

One day, I was just feeling so confused. So disconnected. So far away from myself. You know that feeling when you just can't be at ease with yourself? That's what it was.

My authentic self was confused with the self I was projecting into the world.

So I started writing to talk myself through it. I asked myself *Why am I doing what I'm doing?*

To help people heal as I'm healing.

And that's when it hit me that my actions did not align with my purpose. It's not that I was exploiting my audience. But I was trusting what others were doing more than I trusted what I was doing. Even though the posts I was putting out there were helping people heal, my focus on a subconscious level was to increase engagement on social media.

After I realized that, I could hear myself say *No, no, no! I am not doing this anymore. My purpose is to help people heal. It's always been my purpose. So before I put any content out there, I'm going to reset my intentions until that becomes my* normal *again.* That's why I immediately decided to change gears.

And that's how the Intention mirror came about.

THE INTENTION MIRROR

Look in this mirror when you forget why you're doing what you're doing.

How often do you catch yourself doing something and think *Why am I even doing this? Is it because I want to or because I'm used to it?* Looking in this mirror, you reset your intention based on who you are and what your purpose is. To live an authentic life, it has to align with your true intentions. If it doesn't, you will feel disoriented.

A simple definition of *intention* is: the true reason for doing what you're doing. Imagine your intention as a seed. It's small, but it will grow into whatever it is.

Train your mind to ask itself before you do anything: *What's my intention with what I'm doing now?* For example, *Why are you making that post on social media? Is it because you want to show others that your life is a certain way? Is it because you want to feel validated?* There's no judgment with what your intention is, but just the action of asking yourself brings you awareness and either redirects you or reassures you.

∽

Plant the seed of the tree that you wish to see the fruits of.

∽

THE ESCAPE MIRROR

Look in this mirror when you feel like running away. This mirror is meant to give you clarity on which feeling or emotion you are avoiding. When any intense and uncomfortable emotion knocks on your door, your initial reaction is to want it to go away. Because feeling it is hard and uncomfortable. For example, let's take anger. Let's go back to that moment before I went on stage and gave my speech (Pillar #8). Running away would have stopped me from expressing my anger, my voice, my truth. No matter where I went, staying quiet would have always followed me. Running away would have saved me the grief of putting myself out there and dealing with the consequences, yes. But I would have let myself down.

I wrote the following reflection to combat my urge to run away . . . to start over and not be reminded of everything that happened since I moved to Canada at sixteen:

> So tell me what would happen if you did run away? What would it end? It might take away the presence of some people and how they make you feel. It might take away the feeling of insignificance for a bit. Because you've been basing your significance on someone other than yourself. Something other than yourself. But you know what? It doesn't matter where you go, whatever you want to run away from will be your destination until you fully experience it . . . Until you show yourself that your fear is all a construct of your mind. Until you learn what it's meant to teach you. Until you choose to stop avoiding it. You might think that avoiding what scares you makes you strong. It doesn't. It makes you a prisoner of fear. Being at home means you come from a place of power, not a place of avoidance or fear.

Ask yourself *Which feeling or emotion am I escaping?* Now welcome it into your home, experience it, and allow it to leave your home so you can free yourself of it.

After looking in this mirror, you might want to take a stroll to the Surrender room.

THE "WHO AM I?" MIRROR

Look in this mirror when you want to understand who you are and what you stand for. In any moment of confusion about the authentic you, look in the mirror and ask yourself:

1. Who am I?

2. What do I stand for?

THE UNVEILING MIRROR

Look in this mirror to get insight into the layers you need to lift to see the real you.

1. What is the one label you believe that the world around you sees or defines you by? (I refer to it as *this* in the poem "What Story Do I Tell You?" on page 156). It could be your body,

your personality, your gender, or whatever you believe are the boxes that the world places you in.

2. What's beneath that—the real you?

3. Do you see the real you without the world's seeing it?

4. What scares you from sharing the real you with those around you?

THE REAL-STORY MIRROR

Look in this mirror to gain clarity on reality instead of what you think it is or what you want it to be.

On one side of a piece of paper, write: *What's the story I'm telling myself?* (ego based).

On the other side, write: *What's the real story?* (reality based).

Do you remember that dreadful Monday morning when Noah called me and told me he couldn't talk to me anymore? The story I kept telling myself was *You're not worthy of being held on to*. But was that the real story? Absolutely not. My ego wanted to hold on to the identity I had given myself for so long to give itself a sense of importance. It gave me the story that would reinforce what I'd always believed about myself.

I remember taking out a piece of paper and drawing a line down the middle of the page. On one side of the line I listed all the conclusions I'd made about myself as a result of what Noah had said to me. On the other side of the line I answered each conclusion according to the following questions:

1. Is this true? and even if it were,

2. Is it helpful to believe it?

One of the things I wrote down was *He doesn't think I'm worth it*. In the adjacent column, in response to *Is this true?* I wrote *I don't know*. In response to *Is it helpful to believe it?* I wrote *no*.

This simple reflection can show you that you're seeing yourself and your story through someone else's eyes, through someone else's home, not yours.

THE MOMENT-IN-BETWEEN MIRROR

Look in this mirror to find the quiet, peaceful space between the past and the future: the present.

You know how when you wake up from a deep sleep and, for a split second, you forget where you are, what day it is, what time it is? The kind of sleep that steals you, oh so beautifully, from all the memories and all the dreams you normally have on your mind? How light, how liberating does that moment feel? It's like a fresh blank page for your life.

And then reality starts coming back to you. Bit by bit. It feels like poison is being repoured into you bit by bit as you remember all that's weighing you down. As you remember events that chain you somehow into the past, and future worries that rob you of your feelings of being enough now.

The Moment-in-Between mirror will help you re-create the moment of complete detachment from your past and future. Here are the steps:

1. Sit, stand, or lie down in a silent spot.

2. Imagine the past as sitting behind you.

3. Imagine the future as sitting in front of you.

What normally happens when you do this is that you feel the past and future have inched their way into you and you're so entangled and enmeshed in them, you can't feel or think anything outside of them. It's like two walls are coming closer and closer to you and you feel you're suffocating out of fear of what they will do to you or what they mean about you.

4. While you imagine this state, imagine a protective power around you, emanating from the home you have inside of you, that keeps past and future from touching you.

5. Repeat: *I am safe. I am okay. I am enough. I am worthy. I am not defined by what happened before. I am not defined by what I did before. I am not defined by what might or might not happen in the future. I am not defined by what I might or might not accomplish in the future. I am okay now, as I am. I am at home with myself now, in this moment.*

When you dwell on the past, whether it's regret over something you did or said, or didn't do or say, whether it's dwelling on a past event that no longer serves you (a breakup, leaving a job, moving somewhere, whatever happened), you are choosing to leave your home. You see, we don't just build our homes in other people, we also build them in other times. In times that no longer serve us. Alternatively, you might fixate too much on the *what if* of the future. Your home belongs here and now, with you. It is alive with you. It changes with you. It grows with you. Every moment you live becomes part of you, but the past moments must be left behind you where they belong. The more you carry them, the more your home will become a place you don't want to stay in, because you've allowed past moments to fill up your present space. When you live in past moments, your home falls into despair; it becomes cluttered with objects that no longer serve you; and it weighs you down with its stagnancy.

It's worth noting that this approach is not meant to minimize traumatic events. If you have experienced any form of trauma, please know that while this strategy might help you, it might require quite a bit of repetition before you can detach yourself completely from past traumas and future worries. And you may need to see a professional therapist to help you with this. I personally found that most of the therapy I did, did not help me in releasing my trauma. However, I do remember key moments that gave me a push forward.

As I was leaving my therapist's office one day, I said to her: "I just don't understand how something so small could affect me this much." (I was referring to the gaslighting I went through.) She replied: "Trauma is not what happened. It's how you respond to what happened."

That response shook me for days and gave me so much clarity. So, if you've experienced a traumatic event, please remember that it's not up to anyone to tell you what right you have to feel the event was traumatic. If it left you with trauma, it left you with trauma. And the goal is to heal from it.

6. Now that you're in your home, in a state of at-homeness with yourself, free of the shackles of the past and the future, ask yourself *What would I like to be doing now? What would I like to be feeling now?* and just do it.

THE FOCUS MIRROR

Look in this mirror when you feel distracted. It begins with a simple question: *Why am I not able to focus?* Be honest with yourself. It could be because your purpose is not clear. It could be because you're distracted by your surroundings. It could be because you have a feeling or emotion knocking on your door. It could be that you're doing too many things at the same time. Answering this question as honestly as you can will bring you clarity on what you need to do to regain that focus.

What's enabled me to remain focused with my work is having a plan for my day written out the night before (I found it best to write it the night before to avoid confusion in the morning about what I'm going to do). My plan includes goals and any organizational steps, a rough schedule, and reminders.

For goals, I usually write three major ones, such as: (1) finalize the chapter I'm currently working on; (2) create x number of videos on x topics; (3) review x files. For organizational steps, I go into more detail. For example, under (1) "finalize the chapter I'm currently working on," I write:

1. Finish Pillar 8.

2. Fix any grammatical and structural errors.

3. Consolidate format of pillars.

4. Remove any repetitive ideas.

5. Ensure seamless flow of ideas.

For the schedule, I usually include eating, exercise, grocery shopping, plans with friends, and the like.

And for reminders, I usually write something that will remind me to stay on track the next day.

The plan should be a realistic, doable outline of what you want to accomplish the next day. Remember to do one thing at a time. You're not a superhero for multitasking. Be intentional with your schedule. Make sure you're leaving time for food, rest, any form of physical activity or meditation, socializing, and the like.

Did you think the plan was over? You know it's not.

I can't stress the following enough: *Identify your distractions. Make a list. Remove them. Be alone with your thoughts, and be clear on what is best for you to be doing in this moment.*

If it's social media, get off social media. Remove the apps from your phone if you have to for a day or a week, or as long as you need to. Remember that a "like" or a "follow" doesn't define you. Remember that the constant hit of dopamine is exhausting you. If it's your TV, turn it off.

If it's being always available for others, put your phone in a separate room until you finish your work.

I do this every time I feel I'm being drained without getting any work done. I end up feeling confused and enmeshed in my surroundings. I know it's because I'm allowing my energy to seep in multiple directions. I try to preserve that energy by removing potential distractions before I start working. I usually put my phone in another room, because I know it's my biggest distraction.

SIX

Surrender

∾

You enter this room when you feel an emotion knocking at your door. By entering this room, you drop the resistance to how you're really feeling and give yourself space to feel your emotions. This will let you accept reality and reveal to you all the patterns you fall into when coping with emotions—sadness, vulnerability, shame, anger . . . You might find yourself resisting coming to terms with your emotions, numbing them, or simply denying their existence. Experiencing those emotions will clear out room for new ones of your choice. Part of building a home for yourself is opening the door to experiencing what's really happening on the inside. Emotional exposure to yourself is at the epicenter of this room.

The ultimate goal of being home with yourself is not to never experience negative emotions, but to learn how to dive into them by constructively listening and understanding, not drowning in them by continuing to resist them.

Are you ready to start welcoming your emotions?

Let's walk in.

Surrender . . . surrender to yourself. To what's really going on inside. Drop the mask. Drop the excuses. Drop the resistance. Drop the need to look like you're doing well by whatever standards there are around you. Your family, your community, the world, social media, and so on. This is why the tools in this room are called submissions, not with the weak connotation, but with the opposite-of-resistance connotation.

Just surrender. Don't just *hear* your inner voice. Actually *listen to* yourself. Listen to your heart. Hear your soul. And . . .

Listen to your pain.

Listen to your self.

During the time when I was trying to understand why my need for love was so painful, why I so badly wanted someone—anyone—to love me, I felt like I'd built a home for sadness inside me. I felt sad all the time. I felt less than. You know how a tree extends its roots to wherever water is? I felt like I was extending myself in all directions to get love from anyone, anywhere, with any quality. Just to keep going. I hid my desperation very well while I sought every possible confirmation that I was unworthy of love. And wherever I found those confirmations I convinced myself was a source of love. I was seeking medicine from the pain. Because I thought the pain had more power to change the way I saw myself than I did.

Every rejection, every no, every sign of indifference proved to me I wasn't worthy of love. As a result, I'd run back to those who gave me slivers of their attention and love, even if that came with mountains of toxicity. I was willing to endure abuse to receive a tiny bit of love. It was a feedback loop that plunged me into pits of sadness and despair. And whenever I'd fall into that pattern again,

I'd blame myself for falling again. I'd blame myself for making the choice to go after what hurt me. And I would internalize that as *You deserve to hurt and be let down until you learn the lesson.*

What lesson, though?

Just as I'd lifted layers that stood in the way of me being authentically me in the Clarity room, I also had to unveil myself here. I had to go back to the child who always felt that something was missing. I had to go back and ask why this child continued to believe that home, belonging, love, being okay, was something she could never have. And not just while trying to learn what self-love is. Or who I am. But while also learning why I had this deeply ingrained resistance against . . . something.

Against . . . breaking down.

Against . . . unveiling myself.

Against . . . hurting.

Against . . . asking for what I want.

Against . . . asking for what I need.

Against . . . feeling ashamed of what I need.

And if I could look back at my life and ask myself what this resistance looked like, it would be years of aching to be truly seen, heard, and loved while judging myself for having that ache and veiling it with what I thought was strength.

I kept my ache at the door. Because I was ashamed to admit that I had that ache. I kept it knocking. And over the years, it kept knocking. It kept getting louder and louder until *louder* was just *loud.* Until *just loud* was *normal.* Until I adapted to living with a protective layer around my ache. But here's the twist . . . it's not that the ache was *outside* of me trying to be felt by me. That ache was *inside* of me trying to be seen by me. Heard by me. Felt by me. So while I was carrying it, I was also convincing myself that not giving it my attention would keep it outside of me. Out of sight, out of mind, right?

The ache was inside of me, and the door that it was knocking on was inside of me, too. It weighed me down, but I normalized its presence so I could deny its existence.

~

Denying the existence of anything doesn't erase its existence. It just keeps you in denial.

~

So the ache became heavier. Because on top of that ache, there was an ache for it to go away. There was a judgment on my part toward myself that I even had that ache to begin with.

And that pushed me to become even more homeless.

Because instead of tending to the ache myself, I was seeking to be seen by others before I saw myself. I was looking for others to take my ache away. To fix my ache. To fix me.

I was looking for others to help me carry that ache so it would become lighter. And it would, every time I built part of my home in others. Every time I found a home in others.

But was that fair of me to do?

No, it wasn't.

At the same time, did that give others permission to take advantage of my need for home? No, it didn't.

Forgiving myself meant empathizing with that little girl inside of me and telling her: *Little one, your need for home does not make you any less. It is not a light of permission for anyone to put you down. It is not an excuse for anyone to take advantage of you. Little one, you're just figuring things out. You're just learning.*

So, if I had those realizations, why did I continue to fall into the pattern of building homes in others? I had made strides in my awareness of what love is and what it isn't. But that awareness was not enough. Something needed to *really* change.

As I told you in the Clarity room, there is not one defining moment that will push you to build a home for yourself and never look back. There is a series of moments. Each moment gives rise to new ones until you reach the point where you're completely unveiled and you've built that glorious kingdom within you. So as you're reading, you might wonder why I keep going back to the same stories if I've already had realizations about them. Here's why: *Just as you must unveil multiple layers of yourself, every story has multiple layers that must be unveiled as well.*

Looking at your story from different angles will lead you to the core. And there is no quick fix. You can't just go directly to the root without taking the steps to get there. You might not feel progress at every step, but overall, you do. Think of going to the gym. You don't see progress after a one-hour workout. You see it after weeks of accumulated one-hour workouts. It's the same thing with healing. You might have moments of reflection every single day. You might feel good after some, and worse after others. And that feeling might last for a minute, an hour, or longer. But overall, you can't expect to heal fully in a split second. That moment when you get the revelation that sets you free or makes you truly see the REAL story—that moment doesn't come instantly. And it can't happen without the accumulation of moments of healing.

I also want to show you, by unveiling before you, that there is no shame in taking as long as you need to heal from whatever it is that you're going through. Here I am, opening my heart up to you, bringing you my most vulnerable moments, thoughts, and feelings. This is me. I'm a human being, just like you. And I'm showing myself. I'm surrendering right before your eyes. You might never meet me in person. I might never be real to you. But I'm just like you. I have family, friends, and acquaintances. I have people who hate me. I have people who might read this and pity me, or say *See, I told you something is wrong with her. Do you see how much she dwells on her pain?* And if you think all of that hasn't crossed my mind as I put my words on these pages, you would be wrong. But here I am, surrendering into my ache. Seeing it. Hearing it. And feeling it. Here I am, breaking down the shame that served as a protective shield for that ache and all that came with it. I no longer see strength as hiding the ache. I see strength as opening the door inside of me for it. And whatever that looks like to anyone outside of me is not up to me.

Pillar #1: Welcome Emotion When It Comes to You

"He left me and I feel very sad. He said that he doesn't love me anymore. I don't know what to do to get rid of this feeling. Help me."

"After two years of being together, I discovered that she'd been sleeping with someone else ever since we met. I feel so hurt. I don't know how to stop feeling this way."

"He broke me down so badly and now I'm trying to heal, but it seems impossible. I really want to move on and take this pain off of my heart, but I don't feel strong enough."

"My father passed away and I didn't get a chance to tell him every-thing I wanted to. How do I deal with this?"

I get messages like these all the time.

And over time, I've noticed some common themes:

1. There's an *ache* inside of every person to make the pain go away.

2. There's a *resistance* to feeling the pain.

3. Even worse, there's an element of *self-judgment* for not being able to make the pain go away, or go away any sooner.

That ache to push the pain away, the resistance to actually feel-ing it, and the self-judgment that comes with it . . . all add up to imaginary blocks that stand in the way of that pain's being felt in the first place. So instead of actually feeling the pain, you are more focused on the fact you have to experience it in the first place. It's like the emotion is a river and you're putting a dam in its face. The higher the dam, the higher the level of the emotion, and the more intense the emotion will become. This is how you end up carrying emotional debt. It could be a debt of sadness, anger, fear, or shame. Jump to Pillar #2 (page 210) to explore this further.

SUBMISSION #1: HAVE TEA WITH YOUR PAIN

Do you remember this poem from the Forgiveness room? This will be the basis for our first submission in this room.

When pain knocks on your door:

Let it in.
If you don't, it will knock
harder and harder.
Its voice will become
louder and louder.
So let it in.
Spend some time with it.
Understand it.
Then walk it to the door
and tell it to leave
because it's time for you to welcome
happiness.

The part where I say *Let it in* . . . that's where you stop resisting what the pain demands you to feel. When I say *Understand it* . . . that's where you give yourself permission to identify the emotion. Is it sadness? Is it anger? Is it disappointment? Is it shame? Is it fear? When I say *tell it to leave* . . . that's where you take power by having understanding and consciousness over the emotion instead of allowing it to trap and cripple you in a dark place.

I wrote that poem three years ago. If I could rewrite it, I would title it "If Emotion Knocks on Your Door" to validate both the positive and the negative emotions knocking at the door. So if you need to have tea with a negative emotion, have it. If you need to have tea with a positive emotion, have it.

Give yourself permission to feel the emotion. And remember there's nothing shameful about having to experience it. Don't judge yourself for having something to work through. Sometimes, when it becomes apparent to us that there's an emotion that we have to deal with, we panic and decide to go numb. When I first started seeing a therapist and she brought to my attention certain childhood traumas that I wasn't aware lived inside of me, I did have many moments where I thought to myself *This is going to be so much work! I wish I didn't know about this!* It's like, once you become aware of what you need to work on, there's no denying its existence or becoming unaware of it. So with that comes quite a bit of work to do. And some people just don't want to do the work. Metaphorically, when you open the door within you for a specific emotion, reality hits you that this emotion is waiting to have tea with you. And you go through moments where you regret tending to it in the first place. Because you think that tending to it is what allowed it to be so painful. But that's not true. The pain was there, and it was going to stay until you spoke to it and felt it. Be grateful it was brought to your awareness, because now you can heal it and live free of it. Judging yourself for having that emotion inside of you will not make it go away. Fearing it will not make it go away. It is only once you understand it and listen to what it's trying to tell you that you can allow it to be felt by you. And once you do that, you allow it to leave.

> *We all just want to heal.*
> *We want to rush to Destination Healing.*
> *We forget that healing happens*
> *on the road to healing.*
> *It's in all the roads that you take.*
> *And in all the stops that you make.*
> *It's in all the people that you meet.*
> *And in all the lessons that you learn.*
> *It's in all the scenery that you see.*

And all the mountains that you climb.
Stop rushing.
You miss out on the journey
when you focus on the destination.

Pillar #2: Stop Accumulating Emotional Debt

Did reading that feel like a punch in the stomach? It felt that way for me when I visualized it this way. When I was writing about forgiveness, I kept asking myself *How far back do I have to go?* Because I allowed unresolved pains and traumas to accumulate over the years without actually experiencing the emotions they were demanding me to feel. I had no idea where to start. And because of not knowing where to start, it was very tempting for me to not start at all. It was very tempting for me to close my journal and go hang out with *anyone*. Help out *anyone*. Spend *any* amount of time doing things for others. But I had to come to terms with some realities that I'd been keeping inside of me, in a dark corner that I just wanted to forget existed. You know that room in your house or that corner in one of the rooms where you put things you don't want to deal with? And it's always with the hope that one day, when you have time, you will organize them? And every time you're reminded of it, you have a mini panic attack on the inside? This is exactly the same. The emotions are piling up there.

Let's quickly understand the relationship between feelings and emotions. First, a feeling is a product of the meaning that your brain attaches to experiencing an emotion. For example, disappointment (an emotion) is experienced through feeling that something you hoped would happen didn't happen. Anxiety (an emotion) is experienced through feeling that something bad is going to happen, mixed with uncertainty of what that bad thing is.

Second, feelings are experienced consciously, whereas emotions can be experienced consciously or subconsciously. That explains why sometimes you can't pinpoint what's going on inside of you that's causing a disturbance. Your body experiences the emotion, while your mind decides what meaning to attach to the emotion.

Now imagine what would happen if you allowed your body to experience the emotion, but your mind didn't assign it a meaning because you never took the time to ponder upon what was really happening on the inside. The emotion would persist. Eventually it would control you. That's why it's important to take the time to understand what emotions are being experienced by you—so your mind can assign meanings to them. Only then will you be able to feel them and release them.

So what is the first step in understanding your emotions? Give yourself permission to be human and experience emotions when they visit you. As I was going over the first draft of this chapter, I realized that I hadn't included positive emotions. It was a bittersweet moment to realize how little experience I have with positive emotions. Negative emotions were familiar, predictable, and safe. Whereas the opposite was risky. It was dangerous. And there was an underlying fear associated with accepting that I could deserve the experiences that positive emotions could lead me to.

It is just as risky to experience positive emotions as it is to experience negative ones. But we are more likely to choose the negative ones over the positive ones when we already know what to expect with the negative ones. That's why, for example, those who come from broken homes are more likely to fall into relationships where they experience abuse without seeing it as abuse. It's familiar to them, but that doesn't mean it's not painful.

SUBMISSION #2: EXPRESS YOUR GRATITUDE FOR POSITIVE EMOTIONS

We are more likely to focus on the presence of negative emotions and diminish the positive ones because we fail to take a few moments to also open the door to those positive emotions and *really* feel them, acknowledge them, and be grateful for them. Our tendency to more likely notice the negative than the positive in life is commonly referred to as negativity bias. If you're like this, don't think you're weird or that there is something faulty about you. Evolutionarily speaking, negativity bias served to keep us aware of danger in order to survive. And we've carried that bias with us to this day. Getting past it requires a certain level of going against our nature and actively practicing seeing the positives. You train yourself to look for the positives.

What helped me welcome positive emotions was an exercise my friend Brittany and I promised we would do every day. We send each other a voice note that includes three things we are grateful for. Those three things could be the same every single day. They could be as simple or as complicated as you experience them. This simple three-to-five-minute activity has transformed my conditioning. It has me looking for positive emotions and listening to that knock on the inside and opening the door for it. This is a simple exercise that you can do with others or on your own. You could write it in your journal or speak it to yourself in the mirror.

SUBMISSION #3: CHANGE THE QUESTION

As my friend and I practiced expressing gratitude, we both noticed we'd become more aware of the language with which we were addressing each other. One day, shortly after we began this practice, Brittany told me she'd come across Christie Marie Sheldon's concept of lofty questions. Asking "lofty questions" is a clever way to trick your brain into looking for the positive. Instead of saying to yourself *Why can't I just be beautiful?* you'd ask *Why am I so beautiful?*

Expressing a question as a positive makes your brain look for evidence of whatever you wonder about. Thus if you are wondering why you are so beautiful, your brain will show you evidence of your beauty throughout the day. And if you ask a question as a negative, your brain will look for the negative. It's a genius idea, and you have to try it.

Here is another example: Instead of saying *Why is my life so lonely?* ask *Why am I surrounded by so many people who love me?*

It's your turn. Write down the negative questions you find yourself asking yourself throughout the day, then rephrase them as positive ones.

Pillar #3: Accept What Is, Even While You're Trying to Change It

Part of surrendering is accepting reality. That means properly assessing and understanding where you are now. That means you stop thinking *But it shouldn't be this way*, or *But it should be that way*. Instead you say *It is what it is.*

One of the defining moments in my life was when I realized that the reason I held on to men who were not offering me anything was my ego—that is, the story I told myself about myself, that I was not worthy of being held on to. I had to call myself out on my own hypocrisy. I didn't really love Noah, let alone like him. I loved the validation I got just by him accepting what I had to give. Because that somehow made me feel like what I had to give was worth it, making *me* worth it.

Come with me to a moment with Adam, the guy I started seeing several months after my last interaction with Noah. I'd put that story behind me and was making an intentional effort to stop the pattern of proving my worth to anyone. While taking a walk in the park and discussing past relationships, Adam turned to me and said: "So explain this to me, because I'm having a hard time with it. How do you get attached to someone who doesn't want you? How do you get attached to someone you were never in a relationship with? Because for me, if someone doesn't want me, I don't even try to make them like me."

This is the same question my editor asked me to reflect on when writing about Noah. It's the same question that got me to feel writing was a burden for a good two weeks. Because I didn't want to face it. I was aching, resisting, and judging myself all at once.

The reason that I didn't want to answer this question is because of how afraid I was of coming to terms with what I was *really* thinking. It was easy for me to say *He gaslighted me. He manipulated me. He just wanted attention.* And that's all true.

But . . .

That's not what I was resisting accepting now. I'd already accepted that and felt the pain of it.

But there was a deeper level of emotion I hadn't allowed myself to accept yet. And that's why it's still hidden deep inside of me. That's why I still get agitated when Noah's name is mentioned. Or when I am reminded of him.

I turned to Adam and said: "You wouldn't understand it, because you're a very secure person." (Sidenote: This is very true about Adam. And it's one of the main reasons I was attracted to him.) "I haven't had that kind of security in my life. I've had to prove my worthiness of love to people my whole life."

This was just scratching the surface. I'm getting riled up as I'm thinking about this and there's a tightness in my chest.

I let go of Adam's hand because I feel an urge to run away. An urge to just not open up. *Why do I even have to talk about this?* I think. In the context of this Surrender room, I'm resisting being vulnerable. I'm resisting opening the door to the positive emotion of connection with Adam.

But Adam put his arms around me as he stood behind me. He whispered in my ear: "Can I tell you something?"

"Yes," I said.

I can't make this up. He said "You are worthy of being held on to."

In this moment, I felt my heart crying on the inside. These were the words I'd been telling myself for so long. And you know why I was so upset about the whole Noah situation? Because I let myself down. I felt fooled. I felt I actually knew better. So why was it that I fell for what I already knew was wrong?! I was experiencing a mix of deep humiliation, embarrassment, shame, and insecurity. All these emotions were being experienced by my body, but they weren't allowed a voice. And that's why there was the agitation, the annoyance, the pain and hurt every single time Noah's name or memory came up. I masked all of that by focusing on his faults. Because that was easier.

But to face my own reality? That was difficult. So I resisted it.

Back to where we were . . .

I looked at Adam. I could sense my frustration bubbling to the surface. And I said: "I don't like talking about it because I feel like I let myself down! I'm so ashamed of speaking about it because it sounds so stupid! Why did I hold on to someone who didn't give me any indication other than a few nice words here and there? Why did I hold on to someone who clearly told me that even though he liked me, he wasn't ready? Why did I hold on to someone who often encouraged me to be vulnerable, only to shut me down and tell me that me being vulnerable was too much for him?"

I knew better. But I didn't want to see it. I kept making excuses that fit the story I wanted to see.

Once I accepted reality for what it was (the emotions I was truly experiencing), as opposed to what I wanted it to be (blaming Noah for my pain), that surrender in itself allowed room for my emotions to be felt.

Noah was nothing. He was a nobody. I don't even think I cared for *him*. I cared about how I felt as a result of him being him. And his dismissal of me served my belief I wasn't worthy of being held on to.

And the beautiful irony about dropping the resistance to all those negative emotions is that I was simultaneously dropping my resistance to experiencing a positive emotion—*connection*.

I know that, at this point, you're wondering if there were any developments with Noah. You're probably waiting for the dramatic ending that involves him coming back into my life. There was no such ending. The final ending certainly did not leave room for any kind of closure coming from him. It blindsided me in a way that pushed me to relive a past I believed I had healed from. I spent days, probably weeks, reliving the pain of the moment when he turned from feeling like light to feeling like darkness. I felt like I was saying farewell to the happy ending I'd so badly wanted before it even had a beginning.

I had to learn, the hard way, that when you keep trying to change the ending, it will only end worse than the way it ended the first time. And the answer I'd been in search of for so long came to me when I stopped looking for it outside of myself. Why did an *almost* relationship cause me so much pain for longer than I thought it should? Here was the answer: I was so fixated on the happy ending that I forgot to make sure the right characters were in place. I didn't even make the characters audition for their roles. I was so desperate to get to the happy ending that I just allowed anyone to take any role. And if it hadn't been Noah, it would have been someone like him. Because my happy ending was based on me proving I was worth *that* instead of believing it first. My happy ending was *that*, in the future, based on someone giving it to me. Based on someone building a home for me within him. My happy ending was based in others, not myself.

And, for the longest time, I convinced myself that the story had to end the way I thought I needed it to end. That's why every time it ended, I went back. It was like gambling, except I lost every single time. The truth is that, sometimes, the happy ending begins with someone walking away from you. Sometimes, it's better when they don't give you a reason. As hard as it is, it awakens you to your desperate need to come home to yourself.

I didn't reach this level of resilience, strength, and at-homeness with myself out of nowhere. It was out of the worst moments I experienced. My biggest fear being abandonment, it was the moments of abandonment that pushed me to understand that when you build your home in other people, you give them the power to make you homeless. It was surviving and living through these moments that pushed me to start building a home within myself from the foundation up. Brick by brick. Wall by wall. Pillar by pillar. And I furnished it as I wanted to.

Had those who abandoned me allowed me to rent a space within them, I would have never found the need to build my own home. I wouldn't have tended to the emotions that had been aching to be felt by me. Building a sense of home in other people distracts us from the real work we need to do for ourselves, within ourselves. At the same time, it keeps us from surrendering to the emotions that need to be felt by us.

Pillar #4: Stop Trying to Change an Ending

Some ends are like this and they have to be like this. Why do I dwell so much on endings? Is it because I'm attached to sadness? Is it because I'm not happy with myself? I think that's what it is. I'm not happy with myself. There are so many things that take me down a spiral, including that feeling of not being accomplished enough, like I still have to prove myself. And it makes me question everything I'm doing. I'm reflecting on why it is that when I put work out there, there's a part of me that wants the world to say

"WOW! Look at the great work she's doing!" And it's not out of having too much pride, but out of feeling too small. And I think it's partly because I didn't get that growing up . . . and then I did through social media and writing. And it felt good for once to be recognized and seen . . . maybe "seen" is a better word. And maybe I can't see myself without someone seeing me. And the reason why when I'm sad I think of every person who didn't see me. And it's like . . . I want to change the ending of those stories. So I put everything together. I take all these stories with bad endings, or endings that make me feel like I'm not good enough or don't deserve to be seen or loved. And I put them together and I go into a hole. And I don't know how to get out of it.

I found that in my journal. I remember crying the day I wrote it. That was a moment of surrender.

And while being in that hole felt so dark and lonely, it was exactly what I needed. I wasn't giving up. I was surrendering to reality. I was accepting it. I was seeing it. Because in that state, I could see myself. I could hear myself. I could truly recognize I wasn't seeing myself without someone else seeing me. Without an accomplishment. Without external praise. In that hole, I was feeling the ache. I let go of my resistance to it. I cried instead of staying *composed*, whatever that means. I let go of my resistance to seeing myself and my reality. And . . . most miraculously, I could call myself out on my own self-judgment. And I could look at myself with empathy as opposed to demeaning talk. In that moment of surrender, the truth started revealing itself to me . . . the truth that it wasn't particular people or setbacks or letdowns that I was hurting over. It was the exact same ending that I was hurting over. The ending that each one of those stories and people proved to me . . . that I wasn't worthy. That I was less than. That I was not good enough. Not only was the truth revealed to me, but the level of empathy I spoke to myself with was mind-blowing. It was so foreign to me. Instead of telling myself *You deserved that kind of end,* I said things like *You accepted that kind of end because it's the only end you've known. And it's familiar.*

SUBMISSION #4: WRITE IT DOWN

Write it all out. I believe the beauty in writing is the freedom and liberation in it. Open up to yourself, your pain and emotions, and answer this: How are you *really* feeling? See where it takes you. Here's a tip: Don't worry about the quality of writing. Don't worry about someone seeing your writing. Don't edit. Let it be as it is. The moment you find yourself judging yourself or wondering how your words would be read, push through it, because that's how resistance against surrendering manifests.

∽

*Stop trying so hard to change the ending of
that one story. It's an ending, not the ending.
Especially if it leads you to the same conclusion
about yourself: "I'm not good enough."
"I'm not worthy of being held on to." And so on.*

Don't make the ending of one story the ending of your story.

∽

There are so many pages left in your book

The following poem specifically describes endings in the middle of stories, shocks, and surprises to the happy endings we thought we would have with others.

What might feel like
them ending the chapter
in the middle
is truly their pen
running out of ink,
their heart
running out of love for you,
their home
running out of space for you.
But how beautiful is it
that you get to finish the sentence they left hanging?
That you get to finish the pages they left empty?
That you get to write the ending of the chapter?
How beautiful is it
that you get to

turn the page
and start a new chapter?
A chapter that says:
Welcome Home.
I've been waiting for you.

Part of surrender is in not going back and trying to revise the event that triggered the pain. That in itself is resistance. Accepting the ending of one story means seeing it as part of your journey, not your final destination. That's why some people get stuck for months, years, or sometimes even decades on the ending of one story. They keep talking about how their life would have been so different if that story didn't end the way it did. They get so fixated on regretting what they could have done differently to make it work.

During one of my trips in Los Angeles, I took an Uber to an event I was attending. Strangers tend to open up to me within minutes of our making small talk. The driver, let's call her Linda, was asking me about what I do. I told her that I write. I read her one of my poems on letting go and she immediately said that was exactly what she was going through—having a hard time letting go of someone she loved. It turned out she met the person she believed was the love of her life ten years ago. She still believed it as we spoke. She said the relationship ended because she was too insecure.

"He loved me. But I screwed it up. I couldn't just let things be. I obsessed over him and where he was. . . . What he felt about me."

She told me they were on and off for a few years and the last time she saw him was by coincidence in the park. He was married with two kids. She said that she's still not able to let him go because he was the best thing that ever happened to her.

If misery sounded a certain way, that's exactly what she sounded like. She was stuck living in the past. She said that no one she met ever compared to him. "I always go back to him in my mind. I wonder what life would have been like with him. I wonder what would have happened if I'd done things differently."

This is what I told Linda, and if you're going through the same situation right now, listen to these words: No two people you meet will be exactly the same. If you loved someone, understand that it's okay if loving someone else doesn't feel the same. It doesn't mean that it's wrong for you. It just means that it's new. It may be unfamiliar, and that's okay. Continuing to look for a person from your past in someone new will always leave you feeling defeated. It's not a fair standard to set for the new person. Also, continuing to believe the best of your life happened in the past will stop you from believing that more good will come. And it's all about mindset. When you learn to not make *an* end *the* end, you'll see your life as a series of beginnings and endings that are leading you to your home.

In *Sparks of Phoenix,* I wrote:
All of the places that let you go
are leading you to your home.

Pillar #5: Surrender to the Familiar to Open the Door to the Unfamiliar

If you don't hold on to yourself, no one holding on to you will be enough. The best proof is in how we dwell on every person who "abandoned" us or chose to walk away, and how we push away those who hold on to us. And, yes, we could say that we pushed them away out of fear, but is it truly fear or is it the unpredictability of stability? Is it fear or is it stability that we've never felt before? Stability that's so unfamiliar to us?

When people ask me "Why do I always attract the wrong people?" I always say: "It's not that you're attracting the wrong people. It's your being attracted to people who are familiar to you, those who make you beg for a place to stay, because you somehow think that earning that place will be the happy ending for you. Recognize that ending up with them is not what will bring you happiness. It's you choosing to no longer be part of that story line that will bring you happiness. Take the lead over your own path. Recognize that being at home with yourself is more important than being welcomed into someone else's home. When the path seems too familiar, it's time for you to move in a different direction."

And let me tell you something . . . If what's familiar to you is fighting to be seen, that's not normal. If what's familiar to you is fighting to be heard, that's not normal. If what's familiar to you is fighting to be loved, that's not normal. You need to make being seen familiar. You need to make being heard familiar. You need to make being loved familiar.

SUBMISSION #5: QUESTION YOUR "NORMAL"

Your heart adapts to
pain

just like your eyes adapt to
darkness.

Imagine this: You're sitting in a room at night. The lights are on. You can see everything clearly. All of a sudden, the power goes out. There's not a single thing around you that you can see. It's pitch black. Imagine for a second that you have no electronics around you to use for light.

At first, your eyes see absolutely nothing. But bit by bit, you start seeing shadows of objects. Your eyes start to adapt to the darkness and you can see parts of the room you couldn't see before. You get to a point where you can move around. You might get a bruise here and there, but you can survive.

Now hold onto that feeling for a moment.

Let's go back to that knock that I was talking about earlier. How it became louder. How *louder* became just *loud*. And how *loud* became normal. After a while of living through anything, as bad as it is, you start being able to survive through it. And after a while, you say *If I'm able to survive through it, then I can thrive through it.* And it becomes your normal. Most people would assume that this happens only in abusive relationships. But it happens in relationships of any kind, even your relationship with yourself.

If you place your heart in someone else's home, it will adapt
to the conditions in that home. If you place it in your own
home, it will adapt to the conditions in your home.

So we can also say:

Your heart adapts to
the unfamiliar
the same way your eyes adapt to
light.

I know how hard it is to accept the unfamiliar. You'll feel your body resisting it. You'll feel your body experiencing more pain while you're trying to make the unfamiliar familiar. And that might convince you you're on the wrong path. It might convince you to go back and try to change past endings, the way you always did.

And you'll find yourself, just like I found myself, going back to holding on to the familiar pain of fighting to be seen, heard, and loved, because that pain is more bearable than the pain of dealing with the unfamiliar.

Do you see it now?

It never was and never will be about whether or not someone wants you. It's about understanding that you wanting yourself is your number one priority. So until you see yourself as worthy, someone else seeing you as worthy won't make you feel worthy. You'll keep running to those who will confirm what you already feel about yourself.

Remember when I said that the pain becomes more intense when you try to move toward the unfamiliar, as opposed to just continuing with the familiar? And how that might convince you to revert back to the familiar, as unhealthy as it may be? Feeling that intense pain initially tells you *You're on the wrong path! Turn around!!! We don't want to feel this!!!* But I'm telling you that feeling that pain with that intensity is actually a great sign you're on the right path to your home. It's your own soul crying to you that it is in desperate need of you. It's your own soul crushing itself, burning down, to rise back up from the ashes of the homeless person you once lived as to the home-ful person you want to be.

Metal is put under intense heat to be transformed. Diamonds are formed with billions of years of intense heat and pressure. You will not transform yourself without doing the work. Without surrendering to the pain. Without taking the risk. And trusting that what's unfamiliar at a soul level, but healthy on a logical level, is worth the risk. It's worth the trust.

In the Introduction, I wrote about the time in my life when I knew everything there is to know about self-love but was not applying it to my life. This is the application.

Think of a malnourished kid who's forced to eat a healthy amount of food one day. Their system initially rejects it because it's too overwhelming. It takes time. It takes getting used to eating a certain amount and quality of food.

It's the same thing with accepting what's unfamiliar to you. It takes time. It takes adjustment. It takes understanding that you won't go overnight from believing you don't deserve a home to building it and feeling at home.

When I look back at my life, I see that I learned to survive on scraps of love and attention, to the point where I thought that's all I deserved. And that's why I didn't know any better in my adult years about the whole love, the whole attention I deserved. That's why I unconsciously held on to what was so much less than what I deserved because I thought it was more than what I could ever get. Once I became aware of that unconscious belief, I was able to actively work on what I knew on a conscious level.

SUBMISSION #6: CHOOSE YOUR NEW FAMILIAR

Use this submission to reflect on the familiar thoughts, emotions, actions, and relationships you have. Redirect your energy toward what you want to be familiar to you. This process will allow you to identify the "unfamiliar" just as "unfamiliar," and to not see the "new" as "scary."

Ask yourself (example answers in parentheses):

1. What is familiar to me? (Think of this as *what you feel comes naturally to you.*)

   What thoughts do I find myself falling into? (*I will never achieve that . . .*)

   What emotions do I seek? (Negative ones? Positive ones?)

   What actions do I often commit to? (*I procrastinate. I don't stay focused on one thing at a time. I don't put myself first . . .*)

   What relationships do I have in my life? What realizations have I made about the people I welcomed into my life in the past, the people I currently want in my life, and the people currently in my life. (*I often go after people who are broken or not ready for relationships. The person I want in my life now is not available to me. I usually accept less than what I deserve because I don't want to be alone. I usually build a home in the person I am in a relationship with . . .*)

2. What is unfamiliar to me but needs to become familiar to me? (Think of this as *What do I want to come naturally to me?*)

What thoughts do I want to fall into? (*I can achieve that.*)

What emotions do I want to seek? (Positive ones!)

What actions do I want to commit to? (*I want to do my work in a timely fashion. I want to stay focused on one thing at a time. I want to put myself first.*)

What relationships do I want in my life? (*I want to welcome people into my life who are whole and at-home with themselves. I want to welcome people into my life who are ready to be in a relationship. I don't want to feel the need to have someone in my life to be complete or whole. I want to focus on building a home within myself first.*)

Positive emotions include joy, hope, inspiration, relief, affection, love, confidence, happiness. Now those might sound to you like ones that you normally welcome, but they're often overlooked. You're more likely to generalize negative emotions than positive ones. Surrendering to positive emotions requires recognition and gratitude. If you express gratitude to what already brings you these emotions, you'll start seeing more opportunities to feel these emotions. In a state of at-homeness with yourself, you'll be able to drop the resistance to the positive emotions knocking at your door, waiting to be noticed by you. And you'll be able to let go of the belief you don't deserve to experience these positive emotions as they are.

The best example I can give you is when someone walks into your life who actually treats you right. Someone who doesn't play games. Someone who gives you attention and is considerate of your feelings. Someone who respects your boundaries. The emotion you're resisting feeling here is love, because it's unfamiliar to you. So you push it away. You keep it knocking. Until it goes away.

Pillar #6: Surrender Through Vulnerability

Vulnerability came into my vocabulary in my early twenties. There isn't one specific word in Arabic that translates to it. Most translations include "weakness" as part of the definition. The most common definition I found in my search is "easy to injure." In other words, you're exposed in some way. Something that would normally protect you is not there.

In the Surrender room, vulnerability is key. Opening the door to a negative or positive emotion is important. Admitting you may have let yourself down is important. Admitting you have work to do on yourself is important. Admitting there are people you need to let go of is important. Admitting you could have done better with what you knew is important. Admitting you're consciously blinding yourself to a positive emotion that's at your door is important. It's not weakness. It's courage. And the origin of *courage* is the Latin word *cor*, which means "heart, as the seat of emotions."

How beautiful is it to think that the act of courage, of showing this heart of yours, requires you to expose yourself emotionally? To unveil? To be vulnerable? To be open to injury? Many of us focus too much on that injury part. What if we said that just as you are opening yourself up to injury, you are also opening yourself up to authenticity? Connection? Belonging? Love? Home?

This unveiling, this opening up, can happen on multiple levels, in multiple ways. I've already spoken to you about the time I decided to take off my hijab, but I didn't share the full story with you. So let me take you back to the moment that changed everything for me.

I'm sitting in my deadly silent apartment one night. I don't have a TV. In this moment, I am surrendering to silence. I close my eyes and imagine what a biography of me would say a hundred years from now.

I could see a page, with a picture at top and center. And the first words say *Najwa Zebian changed the world by* . . .

But wait a minute, the picture. The picture.

The picture is shocking.

I am not wearing a hijab in that picture.

And it hits me: I'm not projecting into the world an image of how I actually see myself. This moment feels more like a lightning bolt than a lightbulb going off in my head.

In this moment, I know I need to make this change. This transition. But I don't even know where to start. Have I become weak? What happened to the courage of waking up every morning and choosing to wear it, as I decided to do after that one bus incident?

All of a sudden, none of that seems to matter. In my heart, I know that courage is in taking it off. Not freedom. But courage.

But how do I tell my family? How do I tell my friends? Where do I even start? What are they going to think of me?

In the process of unveiling, not only did I unveil my hair and my body, but I also unveiled myself. I surrendered to the truth. The truth of who I am. Who I was became clear in the mirror. What I stood for became clear in the mirror. Because that change was not as simple as taking a piece of fabric off my head. It wasn't as simple as starting to show skin beyond my face and hands. It was a process of unlinking my goodness as a woman from the way I dressed. It was a process of detaching my worth as a woman from the inches of skin I covered . . . from *physical* modesty. From *physical* covering. From *physical* hiding. It was a process of detaching my worth as a woman from how hard I tried to not involuntarily seduce a man with my body.

Above all, it was a process of surrender.

Surrendering to my womanhood.

Surrendering to my body.

Surrendering to my choice.

Surrendering to my voice.

It was a process of opening the door to myself. So I could see my longing, and feel my longing. It was a process of letting go of self-judgment for wanting to be seen. To belong. To be loved. To be home with myself.

When I took the hijab off, the hardest part was walking outside without wearing it. As I described earlier, I felt naked. I felt exposed. I felt like I was sinning . . . drawing attention to myself that I shouldn't have been drawing. But upon surrendering to these feelings that were concealed as guilt and shame, bigger truths were revealed to me. I wasn't feeling shame because anyone would feel shame with their head uncovered. I was feeling shame because I was taught by my environment (which included religion and culture) and by the Islamic school I'd attended that my body needs to be covered for me to be a good Muslim girl. At the same time, I resisted feeling joy, euphoria, contentment, relief, serenity . . . I couldn't surrender to those emotions, because I associated them with shame.

One of my biggest fears in sharing my story is that I will be blamed for giving those who already have prejudice against Islam or the Arab culture more reason to hate those two. And to respond to this, I will share a memory. One time last year, during an interview in New York City, a woman raised her hand during the Q&A section and said: "Thank you for sharing your story, but I'm a Muslim Middle Eastern woman and many of the things that you said don't resemble my upbringing. And I fear that sharing stories like yours will perpetuate certain stereotypes about our religion and culture." She went on to tell me that she dresses however she wants, and her family is supportive, that she dates openly, and so on.

My answer was something like this: It's never my intention to say Islam is oppressive. It's never my intention to say the Arab culture is oppressive. It's never my intention to paint a certain picture of either. My intention is to share my story. I'm not here to amplify divisive voices of hatred. I'm here to amplify the voices of those who have been an in-between, like I have been. A drifter waiting for someone to welcome her into their home. People experience this kind of alienation everywhere. They belong to different societies, religions, and cultures. It's important to not discount anyone's story because of the affiliations attached to it.

Pillar #7: Don't Mistake Surrender for Stagnation

I have to make something very clear. Surrendering to reality does not mean staying stagnant. It does not mean accepting injustice. Rather, it means seeing reality for what it really is. Just as your goal in the Clarity room is to see yourself and your life clearly, in this Surrender room, your goal is to allow yourself to experience the emotion that comes with surrendering to your own reality. Really experience it.

If I had perceived surrender to be accepting my reality of injustice, I would have stayed quiet. But I didn't. I reported my story of sexual harassment and power abuse. Accepting that what I went through was unjust—that was surrendering to reality. Surrendering to feeling let down. Surrendering to feeling the pain. And once I did, that's when I raised my voice.

∾

To surrender does not mean to stay in your spot and wait for the world to save you. It means to surrender to the world inside of you. To build that home inside of you.

∾

I used to always say things like *I'm grateful for the pain everyone in my life caused me, because I wouldn't be who I am today without that pain.* Now, I reflect on that and see how wrong it was to speak that way. But that's what I knew then. And I am compassionate with myself for believing that at the time and not knowing any better. So let me go on the record and correct myself: Never be grateful for the person who causes you pain. Be grateful for yourself. Be grateful for the endurance you displayed in healing. Be grateful for all the skills you acquired as you healed from the pain activated within you. Never give credit for who you are now to the pain someone chose to throw your way. It's not about them not deserving that kind of recognition. Remember, the focus isn't on them. It's on you. You get the credit for being the strong person you are now.

I want to share with you a teaching I learned through my educational training. It revolutionized the way I respond to anything in life. When it comes to classroom management, we talk about giving the right level of response to a certain behavior. There are low-, medium-, and high-key responses. For example, if a student is chatting while I am explaining a concept, a low-key response would be to maintain a few seconds of eye contact with the student. That way, my reaction is not overblown, and at the same time it serves the purpose of getting the student to stop that behavior. A medium-key response would be to walk over and stand next to that student while I continue to explain. A high-key response would be to send that student to the principal's office.

In this example, what makes most sense is to start with the low-key response and move upward. However, if the behavior was bullying, I know I immediately must escalate to the high-key response. The response, in essence, is directly related to the severity of the behavior, while keeping in mind the end purpose, which is to create a safe learning environment. If we take this model and apply it to experiencing anger, for example, your anger must be at the same level as the stimulus that caused you to be angry. When you allow yourself to react at the same level, you avoid a high-key response to a low-key stimulus, which happens when anger piles up without being addressed.

So how do you assess the stimulus-appropriate response?

SUBMISSION #7: REACT CONSTRUCTIVELY

There is a level of vulnerability and courage in not submitting to your initial reaction. While the knee-jerk response might reflect our ego, surrendering to the real issue at the core is important before reacting or responding. For example, when I first shared a picture on social media with a strand of hair showing, a girl

from my community left a comment that said "Muslim to Mennonite. That's new." A response from me was unnecessary, but
I did respond. That comment agitated me for many reasons. The
insult within it toward the Mennonite community, for example.
The comparison. The label. The stripping away of my identity.
My response kindly reflected this agitation. However, had I taken
the time to think about my response, I probably would not have
responded at all.

Ask yourself:

1. Why does this stimulus (behavior, comment, . . .) really
   hurt?

2. What are my options for responding? List at least three and
   organize them in order of least to most severe.

3. Is it something I need to respond to? You figure that out by
   determining whether your response will actually alleviate the
   hurt it causes.

   a. If yes, what's the most effective (is it powerful?), efficient
      (is it worth my energy?), and constructive (will it effect
      change?) response?

   b. If no, don't respond.

All in all, not only will surrendering open you up to yourself, it
will also teach you to conserve your energy within your own home
and let go of your need to control more than you actually can, in
yourself and in others.

Surrendering allowed me to open up to myself in ways that

transformed how I perceive my relationship with myself and with others. A happy ending I once believed would only be happy with a man entering my life completely changed. When I first started writing *Welcome Home,* I knew I didn't want this story to end with meeting a guy. Most self-development books have that ending of finding the love of your life. But that's not my happy ending. Home is my happy ending. Finding myself is my happy ending. I did meet Adam, yes. Had I not built a home for myself, I probably would've pushed him away. Because he is unfamiliar to me. He is secure. He respects me in every meaning of the word. He respects my time. He respects what I've been through. He respects my boundaries. And not once since we've met has he ever said or done anything with the expectation of anything in return. He communicates— and I mean *really* communicates. He is . . . at-home with himself. I don't know what the future holds. I might build a home with him one day, but that will never make me sell or abandon the home I have within myself.

Every day that goes by, I express gratitude for working toward being at home with myself before rushing to be welcomed into someone else's home. The pages of my journals are filling up with new poetry and reflections on what true love and companionship look like.

> *If you're waiting for someone*
> *to save you,*
> *you can keep waiting*
> *to be picked up*
> *and broken down*

to pieces
over and over
or you can look in the mirror
and say
welcome home.

SEVEN

The Dream Garden

❧

In the Dream Garden, you will spend your time watering your dreams. Regardless of where in the world you live, you are expected to reach benchmarks and have your life figured out by a certain age.

The struggle to "make it" is universal. In this room, I urge you to not fake it till you make it. Rather, live it and it will lead you to where you are meant to be.

As I share with you my story of how I am living my dream, I remind you to stay authentic, original, and true to your story in a world that convinces you there is only one path to success.

Are you ready to start living your dreams?

Let's walk in.

❧

What do you want to be when you grow up?

Tell me no one's ever asked you this question.

And that's where it begins—the obsession with needing to know what your life should look like in the future so you can start working toward it now. When I was in twelfth grade, I was expected to know what job I wanted, which dictated which program I applied to in university.

I asked my mom one morning about what I'd wanted to become when I was a kid. I knew I'd written it in my elementary school yearbooks. I had a hunch it would say "a teacher," but I wanted to make sure.

Sure enough, my mom said, "I don't really remember, but I'm pretty sure you wanted to become a teacher."

I did.

I wanted to be like my mom and dad. They were both teachers. My mom taught English as a second language and my dad taught philosophy and other social science–related high school classes.

They both taught at the same school that I attended until third grade. Then things started to fall apart. I remember one day arriving at school on the bus. I remember seeing police surrounding my dad. I started crying because I knew something was wrong.

Later, I understood my dad was removed from the school because he "did the right thing." He didn't accept seeing corruption and abuse of power. That's all I was told. But what more could I have understood, even if they told me? I was seven years old.

That's the thing about my dad. He is a public servant. It's in his blood. He's never gone against his integrity to serve his own greed. I don't think he had even the slightest hint of greed. I didn't grow up with money ever being an issue, but on the other hand it was also never glorified. We lived a humble life, because both my parents were humble people. They never attached their worth or value to money. Ever. That's why I never did. And never will. And even though my experience as a child was that of feeling so disconnected and homeless, that was never their intention. In their view, they were doing what was best for me, considering the context of our family being split between Canada and Lebanon.

So when I tell you that I wanted to become a teacher because I wanted to be like my mom and dad, it's because I wanted to be like them in every respect, not just do what they did.

After moving to Canada, I kind of forgot about that dream. My parents wanted me to become a dentist. That's not what I wanted. But I turned down my acceptance into a Social Studies program and took the Science offer because that would make my journey toward dentistry easier. I remember my heart breaking as I turned down my Social Studies offer.

After completing my Science program, I thankfully didn't become a dentist. My grades weren't high enough. For the longest time, I saw that as an indication that I wasn't good enough. I know I'm not the only one who equated their worth with their grades. But now I was stuck with a science degree I didn't want to continue adding to. So I asked myself what I enjoyed doing the most. My favorite courses in university were a second-year history of languages course, a second-year history of medicine course, and a third-year genetic engineering course. The first course I loved because it taught me about the globalization of the English language—how that domination has erased not only other languages but entire cultures altogether. And there was a little activist in me that wanted to do something about it. The second course I loved because our professor walked us through the history of medicine through storytelling. I loved that course. And the third course

I loved because it allowed me the creativity to think outside the box and design genes.

So what could I do that brought together activism, storytelling, and creativity? How could I make change in the world? I looked at my options of what to further pursue with my degree. And there it was . . . my original dream: education.

So I applied for a bachelor's degree in education.

Five years ago, if you'd asked me where I would see myself in five years, I would have told you: I see myself as a full-time teacher, married with two kids. At least. And . . . that's it.

Little did I know that the dream I'm now living was a lot bigger than I'd imagined it would be.

During teachers college, I learned, among other things, the history of education, the power of education, the past and current inequities, and the work that needs to be done to ensure inclusion of all students. I felt the activist within me awakening bit by bit. I actually didn't feel school was tedious. I loved what I was learning. I was invested.

My first teaching assignment, with a group of eight Libyan refugees who ranged from second to eighth grade, proved to be a turning point in my dream. All of a sudden, seeing the look in their eyes—the look of *What am I doing here? I don't belong here!*—awakened, again, that activist I knew I wanted to be. I wanted to make a difference for my students. As I started writing short motivational pieces to inspire them to see themselves through my eyes, I was more than just invested in them—I wanted to change education altogether. I wanted to change the way that educators went about seeing their students. I wanted to change the way that students saw themselves.

In hindsight, I was fighting for everything that my sixteen-year-old self wished she'd had.

I was teaching full-time, pursuing my master's degree in education full-time, tutoring seven days a week, and teaching Arabic in Saturday school, and do you know what the first thing I did when I came home was? Not writing my lesson plans for the next day. Not marking papers or working on my assignments. I wrote. For hours. Sometimes I didn't start my work until two in the morning because I had a nagging thought I needed to get on paper.

As I pursued my master's degree in education in multiliteracies and multilingualism that year, I was studying the role of motivation in new-language acquisition. The notion of investment in learning was a prominent theme in all I was learning. Students learn when they're invested in learning, when they see value in what they're learning. And they engage in learning when they see themselves reflected in what they're learning. Students who are learning English are most likely from diverse cultures. So, naturally, I was interested in cultural relevance in curricula. Are students from diverse backgrounds *really* reflected in the curriculum? Are they reflected in policies? Are students given equitable opportunities? (Hint: The answer is no.) I was obsessed with assessing the application of policy in practice. This led me to find that organizations in general, not just schools, usually have everything right on paper but rarely ever reflect what they preach in their practices. Policies related to diversity, inclusion, harassment, and the like, seem to be put in place as a way to protect organizations legally. It's rarely ever because they actually care about the population that they're serving. Or their employees.

Why was I so interested in all of that research? Because I'd lived through the consequences of all of it. I was, and still am, invested in it. I wanted to find answers for my younger self while creating a better future for today's youngsters.

As I was pursuing this degree, I transitioned into the public teaching system. Immediately, I started getting asked to come into classrooms and speak about culture, diversity, and identity. And that was my favorite part of any day. But if you recall from my "What Story Do I Tell You?" poem in the Clarity room (page 156), I always felt that what I looked like was the definition of diversity. Everyone saw culture and identity when they looked at me. But they didn't see *me*.

So, even after sharing what my hijab, religion, culture, and identity were about, I always aimed to tell students that at the end of the day, whatever the labels that they thought differentiated them from others are, it's who they are on the inside as humans that matters the most. I always kept in mind that each of these students had their own third space and that I, as an educator, wanted to tap into that. It's important to be aware of how you're seen and the consequences that come with it, but it's necessary to see yourself as more than how the world sees you. After the incident on the bus when I was nineteen, I became aware that I stood out because of the way I dressed. I knew I was at higher risk to be targeted with hate. But that awareness didn't hold me back from doing the work I wanted to do.

From an equity and inclusion angle, I saw the numbers. I saw the disparities in success rates among students of color and white students. I saw the disparities in success rates between all students in general and First Nations students. From a socioeconomic angle, I saw the disparities in success rates among students who came from middle-class income, upper-class income, and lower-class income families. It's very sad. And I always wanted to do something about it.

I always brought a copy of my book *Mind Platter* with me as I did my substitute teaching, and I'd take the time to read a page or two to the students. I still get messages from students I taught only once or twice, telling me how much of a difference that had made for them.

You might recall, a few months after I'd self-published *Mind Platter*, the TEDx team from London reached out to me, asking if I would deliver a speech as part of their 2016 TEDxCoventGarden-Women event. The theme for this event was "It's About Time." My idea worth sharing was "It's about time to heal," and I titled my speech "Finding Home Through Poetry." It was the first time in my life I'd taken the stage.

It was during this speech that I spoke about the concept of building homes in other people. That idea stayed with me as an evolving dream that I wanted to finish one day. And here I am, doing that now.

Speaking engagements to audiences in the thousands trickled in afterward. Those audiences included entrepreneurs, teachers, and students. The beautiful thing about all this was the diversity of topics I was trusted to speak about.

And you know what the crazy part was? I didn't see any of this as "work." It was what I loved doing. It felt like breathing. It felt like home to me. It felt like I was doing what I was always meant to be doing. Nowhere in my wildest dreams did I think I would be a writer or a speaker. Even when I started writing at twenty-three, I didn't see myself as a writer. To me, that was just me expressing my thoughts and feelings. That was exactly what I did when my friend

Mariam gifted me a handmade journal at age thirteen. I was just expressing my thoughts and feelings, nothing more.

When I ripped up my journal at sixteen because it symbolized to me everything that I wanted but couldn't have, my soul stopped breathing. It was painful to write, so I stopped writing altogether. It was painful to feel. Seven years later, when my love for writing was rekindled, bringing with it a renewed courage to feel and heal as I did that for my students, that journey led me to this moment. Right now. That journey started as me writing to amplify my students' voices. That's when I started breathing again. That's when life started coming back to me. Color started coming back to me. My pen is my weapon. And the battlefield is the world that tells me and anyone out there that they don't belong where they are. That their voice doesn't matter. That they don't matter.

At the beginning of that journey, I still saw myself as a teacher, even after self-publishing *Mind Platter*. My first three books explored a spectrum of emotions and life experiences. They were written from a place of brokenness. An ache for healing. Writing helped me with the process of healing as I allowed my pain to be heard and felt.

My pen led me to unveil the truth of who I am. And on that journey, I unveiled my hair. I unveiled my body. When I decided to take my hijab off at age twenty-eight, I had people tell me *But you built your whole career on your hijab! What's special about you now?* and *I used to respect you when you wore your hijab. Now you're just like everyone else.* And *You could've made a much bigger impact and much more money if you'd capitalized on the struggle of making it as a hijabi author.* I actually didn't build any of my career on my hijab. And I never wanted to. That is what the world saw about me. Staying true to myself meant I was willing to let go of the world's approval of my decision to be authentic with myself.

I'd often wonder, Why is it that my story is only worthy of being read if I visibly looked different? If I carried a label that made me more worthy of being felt bad for? Why is it that my story is only powerful if I had an added distinguishing label? Why is it that the world has to see through so many layers before they see my voice as worthy of being heard?

> *I carry the burden*
> *of all my past identities*
> *as I revolt to be myself.*
> *I don't resemble the identities*
> *I left behind,*
> *nor do I resemble*
> *the ones I'm mistaken to have.*
> *To the world I left,*
> *I am no longer who I used to be.*
> *I am no longer welcome.*
> *And to the world I entered,*
> *I am too different.*
> *I am not welcome.*
> *So I created my own world*
> *where I get to tell myself:*
> *welcome home.*

You see, writing was my revolution against all I thought I had permission to be.

Writing was my revolution against *Why can't I have that?*

Writing was my revolution against my seventh-grade Arabic language teacher failing me at writing and telling me that I don't follow the rules.

Writing was my revolution against being bullied in school for being too sensitive.

Writing was my revolution against people telling me "Stop putting your feelings out there."

Writing was my revolution against "You know you're in Canada. You don't have to dress like that."

Writing was my revolution against "Muslims don't dress like that."

Writing was my revolution against "Good girls don't do that."

Writing was my revolution against one agent telling me "You can't be just a writer. You'll never make a living out of it."

Writing was my revolution against a culture that taught me that a woman expressing her feelings is shameful.

Writing was my revolution against being seen as a label: Muslim. Sinner. Hijabi. The girl who used to be a hijabi. Sell-out. Hypocrite. Liberated. Oppressed. Sheltered. Too young. Too old. Successful. Not successful enough. You name it.

Writing was my revolution against the woman I thought I needed to be to be worthy of being welcomed into other people's homes.

Writing was my revolution against racism.

Writing was my revolution against misogyny.

Writing was my revolution against patriarchal systems.

Writing was my revolution against systemic oppression.

Writing was my revolution against oppression of any kind.

Writing was my revolution against Islamophobia.

Writing was my revolution against all the challenges that my students faced: discrimination, homophobia, bullying, and more.

Writing was my revolution against the boxes society wants to put me in.

Writing was my revolution against the life I thought I needed to live to be "successful" or "on track."

Writing was my revolution against my homelessness.

No, writing was not my revolution.

Writing *is* my revolution. And always will be.

Even with writing this book, I'm aware of the revolution I'm daring to start. I'm aware I'm at a disadvantage for succeeding, for multiple reasons. First, the memoir/self-development space is dominated by white women. The motivation space is dominated by white men. I am neither. And even if I could pass as the first with my physical features, my name gives me away. Given that, I'm doing what I would do regardless. This is me living out my dream.

And as you can see, my plan from five years ago failed miserably. I'm single. I'm not a full-time teacher. I don't have two kids. But I have a life unfolding before me as I revolt against all the chains that are meant to keep me in my place. That are meant to keep me quiet. That are meant to keep me afraid.

When you walked into this Dream Garden, you probably thought I was going to give you steps to finding your dream. I apologize for disappointing you, but this is the one question I won't tell you I know the answers for. I can't answer the question *But how do I know what my dream is?* for you. What I can do is guide you to find that answer for yourself. If I had a list of steps, we would all turn out the same. We would all be doing the same thing. You have to follow what your at-home self tells you. What feels like home to you? This is not about what you're good at. It's about what you enjoy doing.

And if what you enjoy doing doesn't bring you an income, you have to ask yourself what your priorities in life are. You may have to work a job to live so you can spend the rest of your time living your dream by doing what you love. And that's okay. Just don't spend your life believing the validity of your dream is only as important as the financial validation that it brings you.

Following are some lessons from my journey, which I refer to as lanterns because they light up your way, and some tools, which I refer to as watering cans, because once you make a realization, you will water the ground beneath it.

Lantern #1: Seeing Your Dream Requires You to Unblind Yourself to the Truths Around You

Sometimes a truth is hitting us right in the face and we choose not to see it. Because we are wearing shades over our eyes that blind us to that truth. Those shades place limits on your potential because they are stopping you from seeing that potential, seeing its value, or realizing your ability in achieving it. Had I not opened my eyes to my own potential, I wouldn't have taken any of the opportunities that came along, because they didn't serve my original dream of being a teacher. Speeches at schools or on stages would have been taking me away from my original dream of teaching. They would have been considered a waste of time, a distraction. But I chose to see them as teaching in a bigger classroom, the classroom of the world.

WATERING CAN #1: UNBLIND YOURSELF

What do you need to unblind yourself to?

This is an open-ended question. I want you to look deep inside of yourself and ask yourself about those little moments when you day-dream about the possibility of something. The moment when your brain jumps in and says *But you've already spent so much time on this goal, this dream, this career, this relationship, that everyone will laugh at you. No one will believe in you. Who do you think you are to achieve that? To get there?* All of this . . . that's the process of blinding. And what you're using to blind yourself is:

- Your limiting beliefs about yourself
- What others think of you
- Your fears
- The potential you think you have
- (Insert your own)

Personally, the possibility that I found myself daydreaming of was being heard . . . of living in a world where my emotions mat-tered. Where my story mattered. And the truth that I failed to see for a long time was the one that was screaming to me: YOU ARE A WRITER! Why didn't I see it? Because I'd planned to be a teacher. I wanted to be like my mom and dad. It was a safe option. I knew what it looked like. Whereas with expression and writing, there was no predictable future. There was no predictable outcome. No one around me had taken that path. What was blind-ing me was:

- What if I fail?
- What if I can't make a living?
- What if people don't like my writing?
- But I love teaching.

Now that you've identified how you're blinding yourself and what you're blinding yourself to, what is clear to you about your dream? What is screaming at you? What is the dream that is emerging before your eyes?

Lantern #2: Take It Step by Step

You don't have to have your dream figured out before you live it out. That's the mistake most people make. They draw out a vision for what they want, and they get fixated on reaching that specific vision. While some see that as determination, I see it as drawing a box around yourself and telling yourself that's the only thing you can achieve. Don't get me wrong, setting goals in life is important. But the *how* is something you can't figure out before you start. And there isn't a hundred percent guarantee you'll reach the goal you initially set your sails for. The best stories you hear are the ones that happened so uniquely, that were so unplanned for.

If I'd been so fixated on my dream to be a teacher, I wouldn't have spent any time compiling my writings to put them out to the world. I wouldn't have taken the time to figure out how to self-publish. I wouldn't have taken every opportunity that came my way screaming to me YOU ARE A WRITER. I would have rejected all those moments as distractions.

Being so fixated pigeonholes you. And while that works for some, it doesn't mean it will work for you. Especially if you're reading this book, I know that you're looking to live out your most authentic life. And that includes a dream or a goal that allows you to be your authentic self.

∽

If you look at yourself as a flowing river, not a stagnant pond, everything changes. Imagine that, like a river, you are flowing as you move and live your dream. As long as you keep living that dream, you'll reach a big ocean where the little ripples inside of you become big waves and tides. You have to see your journey of reaching your dream that way. So what might seem to you like a small step will eventually lead you to a bigger one and bring you closer to the glory ahead.

∽

WATERING CAN #2: TAKE THE NEXT STEP YOU CAN TAKE

Instead of being so fixated on the end goal, what are you interested in now? What can you do now? You can't jump up a staircase to reach the top step. You might not even know what's at the top of the stairs. Either way, getting there doesn't happen by you wanting to be there. Getting there happens by you taking the next step you're able to take.

Personally, the first step I took was this: Every time I got the urge to sit down and express myself, I did. I had no fixation in my mind on where that would lead me, whether it would be "worth it," whatever that means, or whether it fit into the bigger picture of an end goal. My goal was to express myself. So if the dream that is revealing itself to you is, for example, art-related, the first step could be to buy paintbrushes, paint, and a canvas. If your dream is, for example, culinary arts–related, the first step could be to start experimenting with simple recipes. You see where I'm going with this. Don't let the illusion of the importance of a big end goal stop you from starting simply and on a small scale.

Lantern #3: Originality Will Set You Free

Don't look at what others are doing and then do what they're doing in hopes it will give you the life that they're living. Being in a state of at-homeness will definitely rid you of your perceived need to make a certain amount of money, reach a certain level of fame, or achieve a certain level of idolatry by others. Don't allow someone else's life to set the bar for your success.

You might enter your Dream Garden as a result of feeling withdrawn or "less than" because someone else attained or achieved something that makes it look like they're happy or successful. Some would define this as jealousy, but I don't see it that way. I see it simply as comparison. And when you compare, there's always going to be someone who has more and someone who has less. "More" and "less" are relative based on what you feel about yourself. And the saddest part is that, if you haven't built that strong foundation of your home of self-acceptance and self-awareness, you are more likely to feel that you are "less." Not that you *have* less, but that you *are* less. Remember that the foundation is crucial because it allows you to know yourself. And when you know yourself, you'll know your worth, who you are, and what you want in life. When you know that, you can't possibly allow the life of someone else to be the rule book for how you live yours.

Why would you even want to walk in this garden if you're going to spend your time trying to mold yourself into someone else's dream? You'll end up feeling, a hundred percent of the time, like a failure. And you'll steer away from this garden because it will make you feel small.

Think of all the times you were driving and stopped to ponder how beautiful some people's homes looked. The thought of owning a home like that probably brought a smile to your face. Our lives and ways of thinking are interconnected. You don't just feel a feeling like that when it comes to seeing physical houses. You also feel that way when you look at the external lives of others, whatever that external part is. Bottom line is, we often admire the homes of others and want to build ones that look just like theirs without even entering them or knowing what's inside. Without even knowing whether they are present in their own lives or not. While you might admire someone's life from the outside, they might be—actually, they most likely are—admiring someone else's life from the outside as well. So you chase the happiness or success someone else looks like they have, while they chase the same thing from someone else. And when you define an achievement by comparing yourself to others, that achievement will be nullified as soon as you find someone else you want to be like. And it goes on and on. And that's why we often find inspiration in the simplest definitions of happiness from those who've lived longer lives than us. They usually remind us to slow down and enjoy the moment. To not rush. To say no. To not care what people think of us. To take risks. To hold on to those who love us dearly, truly, respectfully.

And if you're thinking *But I want to make an impact like so and so,* remember that it's not up to you to pick the impact of your dream. You do what you can do to the best of your ability, and the outcome will reveal itself. Most people are overly fixated on the external validation of their dream. That itself is building a home in a dream instead of building a dream in your home. And I urge you not to fall into the trap of performative activism just for the recognition. The world is now flooded by that for "likes" and "follows." Don't go against your authentic self. Do your work because it's right, not because it'll get you praise or external validation. You don't know whose life you will change with your work, and that shouldn't be the focus. Don't define what the journey says about you based on the destination you reach. You find your meaning through the risks you take, the dreams you dare to work on, and all that you achieve along the way.

WATERING CAN #3: BE ORIGINAL

Originality is a reflection of your authenticity with yourself. With whatever it is that you are creating, always ask yourself the following questions:

1. *What is my intention for doing this?* (This is not to get fixated on the end goal, rather to reflect on whether your intention is motivated internally or externally.)

    a. Am I comparing myself to someone else?

    b. Am I competing with someone else?

2. *Is this original or am I copying someone else?* (In other words, am I following someone else's path to get to the happiness they seem to have?)

3. *Is this me building my home in a dream? Or is this dream within my home?* (In other words, am I basing my happiness on the potential outcome of this, or am I deriving happiness through its execution?)

In a state of being home with yourself, your intentions of living out your dream are internally motivated. They are self-fulfilling. The act of living your dream out itself is validating and further motivates you to keep going. Living out your dream authentically is not driven by where you stand compared to someone else. It's not a race with someone. It's a journey with yourself.

Lantern #4: Living One Dream Doesn't Mean the End of Other Dreams

Many people believe that transitioning from one dream to the next makes the one before it a waste of time. During my master's program in education, we learned about transferable skills between languages. You might think that a student's first language hinders their acquisition of a new language. However, research shows that when a student learns a new language, the skills they learned in their first language are used to bridge the gap between both languages. It's the same thing with dreams.

Why am I telling you this? Because you might find yourself believing that living out a new dream negates all the experience and knowledge you gained from past dreams. This is only as true as you allow it to be. Throughout your life, you will gain skills that are useful across diverse contexts. These skills could be organizational, analytical, managerial, and so on. Use whatever you can of those skills toward your new dream.

I went from teaching within a classroom to teaching within the world. I took all I learned in my university training and teaching and applied it to teach people about healing. You can do that, too. With whatever transition that you're making.

When my writing took off, I was still teaching and enrolled in my doctorate full-time. I knew at that point that writing was my calling, but how could I leave this job that I'd worked so hard for? After four years pursuing a bachelor's degree in science, a year getting a bachelor's degree in education, a year getting a master's degree in education, and two years working toward a doctorate in education, and at a time when I'd already landed a contract in the public education system, I decided to transition into my passion—writing. I remember everyone around me telling me how crazy I was to be walking away from what I'd spent eight years pursuing. They reminded me of what a waste it would be to just let go of all that schooling to pursue writing.

The turning point for me here was this: It could be seen as eight years wasted, or as eight years invested in preparing myself for the best career I could ever have—truly helping people change their lives. It could be a lifetime of staying in this job because of the eight years I'd invested, or seen as the learning opportunity I'd needed to enable me to pursue my real passion. Instead of seeing what you've done for a past dream as a waste when you decide to pursue a new dream, look at skills and tools you gained and can now use to propel your current dream.

WATERING CAN #4: MAKE THE TRANSITION

Making a change doesn't mean you wasted time on what you did before. If you perceive it that way, you'll only waste more of the time you could be using to pursue this change.

What skills from past dreams can you transfer to your current dream?

A few of the skills I transferred from my education schooling and teaching are:

- Never assuming that someone knows what you're talking about.
- Using simple language.
- Making the learning relevant to the experience of the learner.

Now it's your turn to answer the question.

Lantern #5: You Don't Follow Your Dream— You Live Your Dream

If you look at my journey, it'll be clear to you that none of what I was chasing after, whether it was the woman I thought I needed to be or the degree I thought I needed to have, got me here. It was what felt like home to me that got me here. But this is not a call for you to wait around not taking action until you know what home feels like to you. This is a call for you to take the next step you can take. What interests you? What do you feel invested in? What change do you want to make? Figure that out. A small step has the potential to lead you to another small step. And another small step. Until it all comes together and you understand why it all happened.

One theme that pops out at me from my journey is that everything really does happen for a reason. I can't say that my years of education went to waste because I didn't end up pursuing education full-time. Those years led me to be standing in front of eight students who rekindled the flame of writing for me. And that led me to put a book out there. And another book. And another. And now this one. I can't say that moving to Canada at age sixteen shouldn't have happened because of the displacement I felt. That move led me to falling to the depths of loneliness and isolation so I could understand it and better write about it in the future.

One of the first courses I took in working toward my doctorate explored the different types of leadership. The one that appealed to me the most was servant leadership. It's when you serve the people you lead, instead of the other way around. I was called to serve. And I answered the call. Not answering the call would have been detrimental to me. Because I had more to give than I believed I did. And in the process of giving what I had inside, I discovered that my dream was bigger than I ever thought it would be. It was bigger than me.

Everything I lived led me here. I lived my dream. I didn't follow it.

WATERING CAN #5: LIVE THE DREAM, DON'T CHASE IT

Ask yourself: Am I chasing a dream? Or am I living it?

As long as you're in a state of chasing after something, this current moment will feel deficient in some way. You will feel deficient.

Don't base your success on a moment in the future. Let your success be in the now. In every step you take right now.

Lantern #6: Fear of Failure Only Hinders Your Dream

Failure is the word that stops most of us from taking the first step or the next step toward any of our goals. It manifests itself as fear. Most of us can't identify what that fear is of. We just get really anxious before taking a step. That anxiety used to paralyze me. When I was in university, I was so afraid of presenting in front of my classmates that I would actually become physically ill in the days leading up to my presentations. Every time I had an exam or submitted an assignment, that looming anxiety would persist.

I felt that same anxiety before I went on stage to give my TEDx talk on building a home within ourselves. When I think back on it, what was I really afraid of? Was I really afraid, or did I mistake the courage to be vulnerable with being in a state of fear? I now believe it was the latter, but at the time, I believed it was a mix of the two. You see, our minds are so resistant to novelty, to change, that they will mistake the emotion attached to change as *This is not good. Stop. What will they think of you? You'll regret this tomorrow.* That's what paralyzes you. So what is that fear really of? If it's fear of failing, what would failing mean to you? What would it mean *about* you? Is it shame you're really experiencing? You might need a detour to the Surrender room here. Most people who've accomplished success in their lives will tell you they failed miserably and often. If you see something not working as "failure" because of all the meanings about yourself you attach to it, you will stop. But if you see it as *This is what not to do* or *This is what I need to improve,* you'll see it as a lesson, a stepping-stone. And you won't associate it with who you are as a person. You won't care about how others perceive you as a result.

Some might say that living your dream requires both failure and success. I prefer to say that living your dream is a dance between giving and taking. Sometimes that giving includes giving your time, energy, emotional labor, vulnerability, hope, and more in pursuit of living that dream. Sometimes giving means trying multiple times. Trying new things. Learning from errors and doing better the next time. And sometimes that taking includes seeing the fruits of what you invest flourish. Sometimes it includes financial gain. The possibilities are endless. The bottom line is this: You cannot focus only on what you are gaining from pursuing your dream. You have to be willing to give. You have to be willing to risk something, lose something, learn something.

WATERING CAN #6: REPLACE "FAILURE" WITH A NEW WORD

Think of *failure* as a word you need to throw out of your dictionary. It's not failure. It's learning. It's risking. It's investing. It's . . . living. If you base your success on what you get in return for what you put forward, you will see living your dream as failure. And if you base the value of your dream on how the world around you sees it, you will feel an added pressure to "succeed." Focus instead on the journey living your dream has provided you. When you make this shift in mindset, what words will you replace *failure* with?

Lantern #7: Your Dream Nourishes Your Home

Since most people mistake a dream job, degree, life stage, or the like for their "dream," they fall into the trap of thinking they should sacrifice whatever it takes to reach that dream, even if it means that other areas of their life have to suffer. That's a big problem. What's even worse is that many people spend their life working hard, or "hustling," without knowing whether they actually want what they are chasing after. Your dream should serve to support the life you're living. When you equate the value of your dream with the hope of what it will bring you, you are likely to allow other aspects of your life to suffer. Your dream lives within you and allows you to execute who you really are and project that self into the world. The dream you live, whatever it is, should always nourish your state of being at home with yourself. When you look at your life holistically, your dream should not be hindering any primary components of your life, such as your mental health, relationships, or goals.

The illustration on page 264 is a tool I want you to use when you're figuring out if the dream that you are currently living, or pursuing, is worthy. Under the flowers, write down all the important elements in your life, in your home. Now, if you were to imagine that dream or goal in the cloud . . . if that cloud were to start raining, would it nourish those flowers? Would they grow? In other words, as you live out those dreams or goals, are the elements of your home being nourished? Are you being nourished as a person? Are you growing?

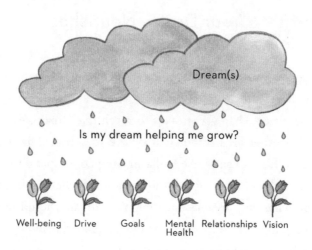

WATERING CAN #7: ASSESS THE
HOLISTICNESS OF YOUR DREAM

When I first started writing this book, I didn't think I would add a dream room. But the more I wrote, the more necessary I knew this room is. And I realized that the room requires time, care, and attention—more like a garden than a room. A garden is exposed to the outer world, as are most jobs and dreams. That's why, most times, we define the value or worth of jobs and dreams by the value or worth the world gives them.

I will end this chapter by reminding you of this: Your dream is made of little revolutions against all you ever thought you had permission to be. Begin the revolution. Don't wait for the right time. Don't wait for the right place. Don't wait until you're ready. Because you never will be. You have to be willing to make mistakes. To fail. To fall. To break. Because on the other side of that, there is your rise. And there is your dream.

EIGHT

The Art of Listening to Yourself

❧

This is not a separate room in your home. Listening to yourself is an integral part of every room in your home. Tuning in to the voices within you is an art that amplifies your thoughts and emotions and allows you to separate your at-home self from those voices. You are not who they tell you you are. You can disarm their power over you by being the listener and the watcher over them.

Listening to yourself is an art that takes practice.

I will now walk you through examples of how I practiced this art in each room.

Are you ready to start listening?

Let's explore this art.

❧

When I initially planned out this book, I had a separate room for silence, with the intention that you need to practice silence in order to listen to yourself. However, the need for silence exists in every room. Silence is a universal language. We all express it, no matter where we were born or raised or where we live. Silence is one of the most powerful languages because of the level of expression and power it can convey. However, it can also be one of the most defeating.

When you are silent within, you can listen to yourself. And as you apply and practice any of the tools in any room, listening to yourself is absolutely essential. Maximizing the power of listening to yourself cannot happen effectively without silence within. What that silence within looks like is tuning in to yourself internally. So you could be, in the physical sense, in a loud place but be silent within, because what you're choosing to listen to is your own voice. To maximize the benefit of walking into each room, you must master the art of listening to yourself.

So, how do you master listening to yourself? It's simple. You master listening to yourself by *practicing* listening to yourself. And you make it a daily practice by setting the intention to listen to yourself. If you have a certain health and fitness goal, getting there doesn't happen by accident. You have to work at your goal every day to see results. Over time, you get better and better as you learn new techniques and gain more and more strength. The hard part is getting yourself to do the work every single day. Setting your intention is where it starts. It's the same thing with silence.

There are three types of silence:

1. *The silence you give others when you listen to them.* For example, when a friend comes to you with a problem, you listen empathetically to make sure you understand where they're coming from.

THE ART OF LISTENING TO YOURSELF

2. *The silence you express to others when you want them to listen to you.* I'm sure you can relate to the following scenario: You sense the person you're speaking to isn't listening to you, so you decide to choose the language of silence because you feel you've used enough words. I'm not talking about giving that person the silent treatment, which implies using manipulation as a weapon. I'm referring to silence that reinforces a boundary, silence that serves to express the value of your words. We can become so fixated on making sure people understand what we say and how we feel that we end up repeating and repackaging it in different words—often because we're looking for an answer or a solution within other people. In a state of silence within, you don't *depend* on others to change your situation. That someone isn't listening to you doesn't affect your sense of self. Your internal reactions are heard by you and understood by you. So you understand that the more you say something, the less impact it has on those who don't want to listen to you. To them, your voice becomes just background noise. It's a silence that values your voice, not a silence that belittles someone else.

3. *The silence you experience within yourself.* This is straightforward. This is the silence you experience when you've turned inward toward yourself.

If you're an empath like me, you've mastered the first two types. They're the ones that we usually get fixated on, because they're focused on others. But, remember, you are no longer building homes in other people. You're building your own home in yourself. So, in this case, the third type of silence is the most important. In this type of silence, you can finally hear the voices within you—even the ones that express negative emotions. This is key, because once you hear those voices, you're able to talk back to them. I used to not be able to fall asleep without the TV playing in the background. Looking back on that, I know it was because I knew reality would hit, and I just didn't want to hear any of my thoughts. But of course it was imperative to hear my own thoughts.

If you master the art of intentionally listening to yourself, you automatically master the art of intentional silence with others. You will also no longer hide behind silence when you want to speak up for yourself. In other words, you choose silence instead of allowing silence to be forced upon you.

Let's go back to intentionally listening to yourself. Why do we shy away from silence with ourselves? It's because silence with ourselves requires us to be alone with ourselves. Alone with the voices within us. And we are afraid of that. We are so afraid of being alone because we equate it with loneliness.

The first time I experienced silence in the physical sense was when I moved out of my parents' home. All the sounds and distractions were gone. At first, the silence was agonizing. I couldn't handle it. It was uncomfortable and unfamiliar. I felt something was missing. I felt lonely. I could hear the negative thoughts taking over, and I didn't know how to calm them. And that's why, even when I had the physical parameters of my own home, I was still homeless. Because I was still not building my own home within me.

Today, I am still living on my own in that same apartment, but now that I've built my own home within me, I find myself craving that time alone. I find myself feeling out of place among others instead of always needing to be welcomed or validated by them. And that's great, because it's allowed me to make the choice to walk away from people or groups of people I don't have a genuine connection with. Over time, silence, in both the physical and the internal sense, has become therapeutic. It's now comfortable and familiar.

Silence within has actually made me a stronger person, because now I can listen to myself. Silence felt uncomfortable before because it made louder the voices I didn't want to hear. It made room for emotions that had been out of my awareness for so long. Now I can speak with more conviction because I know myself better. Listening to myself brought my ego into my awareness and allowed me to become an observer of it. As a result of tuning in to myself, I made some of the biggest changes in my life—changes I would not have made had I still lived in my parents' home.

Taking my hijab off was one of those changes. For the first time in my life, I gave myself permission to contemplate whether the life I was living was one I would choose for myself. For the first time in my life, I gave myself permission to be introspective and question who I really am and what I really stand for.

❧

*Silence within serves as a magnifying glass,
as a mirror, as an amplifier for the voices that
visit you in the form of thoughts and emotions.*

❧

The goal is not to always be in silence, but to use silence as a tool to listen to yourself and consequently understand yourself. Once you master the art of intentionally being silent on the inside, you master listening to yourself. And once you master listening to yourself, your state of being at home with yourself will become stronger. Because you no longer feel the need to make sense of yourself, your thoughts, or your feelings by sharing them with someone else. You hear yourself. Practicing inner silence means that instead of immediately bringing your thoughts and emotions to the surface and speaking them to others, you practice being in a state of listening to them on your own.

Just as not everyone who hears you actually listens, you don't always listen to what you hear on the inside either. Sometimes you know something is wrong for you, but you choose not to listen to yourself. In the same way, sometimes you listen to the voices within you that bring you down. Either way, the answer is not to always ignore the negative voices or to always listen to the positive ones. The answer is to listen to both and to remember they are just voices. You are the one in control of whether you believe them or not, of whether you act upon them or not.

Think about the difference between putting a show on your TV or phone for background noise versus sitting in front of your TV and intently listening. Will you pick up the same information from the show in both scenarios?

The next time you watch or listen to anything on your devices, notice how clean the audio is. The voice of the person you're intended to hear is usually crisp, amplified, and clear. It's not overridden by loud background music or noise that distracts you. It's the same thing with any voice that originates from within you. If you don't tune in to it and intentionally try to listen to it, you miss allowing what it's telling you into your awareness. If you tune in to it, you're bringing it into your awareness.

More often than not, once you tune in to that voice, you will realize that it's stemming from your ego, which serves to confirm the false story you learned about yourself at a young age. And that's a tough voice to listen to. I often get asked *But how do I differentiate between my ego and my authentic self?* The ego is the voice that sounds like a broken record, always trying to make conclusions about you or the world around you. It confines you to labels. It's always trying to stop you from doing something by scaring you with potential negative outcomes, or by pushing you to do something in order to achieve a certain outcome you've attached your self-worth to.

Your authentic self, on the other hand, doesn't jump to make conclusions about you or the world. Your authentic self is the watcher of your thoughts and the manager of them. The ego puts you in a reactive mode because you feel threatened in some way. When my four-year-old niece throws a tantrum because her sister took a bite of her food or because someone interrupted her nap, I could easily overreact and make it about me. But I don't. I also don't just walk away. I come down to her eye level, hold her as she's crying, and validate what she's feeling. I deal with my ego the same way.

My authentic self deals with the ego as a little child having a tantrum, which represents me as a child forming that story about myself, and I observe it. I tell myself *I am not my ego. I am aware of it. I can choose to believe what it tells me about myself. And I can choose to say I see where you're coming from and I see where you're taking me, but I'm not going with you.* Once I do that, I know I've elevated myself to an at-home self, which is sometimes called the higher self. Your at-home self is not at home because it ignored your ego, but because it listened to your ego.

When you listen to your ego, you take away its power. You disarm it. We did the same thing in the Surrender room. When you take the time to open the door within yourself to the pain that's causing chaos by knocking louder and louder, now, instead of that voice having power over you and unconsciously controlling you, you're welcoming it into your awareness. And once you do, you're the one in control.

The most powerful voice you can hear within yourself is your own voice. The voice that stems from your authentic self. And if you spend too much time ignoring it, drowning it out with other voices, you don't recognize it anymore. These voices include your ego, the opinions of people around you, social constructs, and on and on. When you drown your authentic voice by listening to the voices of the world around you, you might be fooled into believing their voices are your authentic voice. It's like listening to a song on repeat and memorizing it to the point you don't even have to think of the words or the tune anymore. The words naturally slide off your tongue.

For example, I went through a phase where I believed my lips were too thin. That's what I would see every time I looked in the mirror. For the longest time, I didn't question where that belief came from—I just believed it to be true. But once I took time to understand why I saw it that way, it quickly became clear to me that the current culture defines big, plump lips as beautiful. And it associates small, thin lips with not being beautiful. But is that actually true? And is it true for everyone? Why can't both be beautiful? When I sat in silence and brought the internal voices to my awareness, I was able to trace them back to their origin. Only then was I able to speak back to those voices and remind myself that I have a choice in how I speak to myself and what I believe about myself.

I'm sure that, as soon as I brought up lips, you thought of some physical feature of your own you are insecure about. Give yourself permission to question where the voice that makes you insecure is coming from, and make the choice to stop listening to that voice. Listen to your authentic voice. Speak to yourself in a way that demonstrates the self-love you know you deserve.

What if you were to write your own song? Your own lyrics? Would you sing them enough times to memorize them and make them naturally slide off your tongue?

If you're an empath like me, you've probably mastered the art of listening to others a long time ago. You know that listening to someone with empathy requires that you listen with the intention of understanding, not with the intention of responding or comparing or belittling. You must listen with the intention of stepping into the other person's pain with them. As you build your home within yourself, and as you live in it, you must master the art of listening to yourself in precisely that manner.

And, remember, the goal of listening to yourself is not to find an immediate answer to your question or solution to your problem. The goal is to *intentionally* listen to yourself. The goal is to tell yourself *I understand you. I see you. I hear you. This is hard. This is a challenging situation.*

Remember: *Practicing the art of listening to yourself begins with intending to do so.* Notice how you react internally to what happens on the inside. What are the first thoughts that come to you? What are the thoughts that consistently come to you?

For the rest of this chapter, I'll be walking you through some examples of how I listened to myself in making my way home, in order to give you some insight into how you can go about it, too.

In the Introduction, "The Road to Home," after things ended with Noah, I wrote:

> "I don't understand why this always happens to me . . . it hurts so much . . . my heart actually hurts. I'm going to need to take some time off. I can't focus on the work we agreed on."
>
> . . . My whole being was preoccupied with this pain. This was bigger than Noah. It quickly spiraled into overblown feelings of abandonment, neglect, and worthlessness.
>
> It was the weirdest thing ever. I heard myself saying *Why are people always so okay with not having me in their lives?*
>
> I was taking an active part in degrading myself. I was telling myself *Who do you think you are?* I thought I'd already done the internal work to change the answer from *I am a nobody* to *I am Najwa Zebian.* How could it be that the answer was now back to *I am someone who's not worthy of love?*

Do you see the moment of awareness? I caught that voice within me. I caught my ego, which wanted to tell me I was unworthy. The act of bringing that voice into awareness was more than enough for me to be aware of it as opposed to believing it.

Moments before I took the stage for the first time to give my TEDx talk, I took a deep breath and told myself *Forget your script. Say what your heart needs to say.*

Had I not listened to that voice, this book would not be here today.

In Chapter One, "Building a Foundation," I described the process of knowing who your authentic self is by listening to yourself.

Anchor #1: Bring Your Authentic Self to Your Awareness

STEP 1. Sit in a place by yourself, in silence.

STEP 2. Listen to what your inner voice tells you. This very likely is not your own, at-home voice. It is likely your ego, which is your sense of self that began to form during your earlier experiences in your life. It is also likely the voices of others and what they've been telling you about yourself. Once you're aware of this, you can imagine pushing those voices away because they really don't define you. You define you.

STEP 3. Tell yourself: My authentic self is not this voice. My authentic self is listening to this voice. My authentic self transcends time and space. My authentic self is not dependent on the labels or definitions that I attach myself to. It is not dependent on my surroundings, people, or things.

STEP 4. Affirm: My authentic self is worthy of my own acceptance.

IN CHAPTER TWO, the Self-Love room, I spoke about being the "CEO of you." One of the strategies I described was meditation. I acknowledged the reasons I thought meditation wouldn't work for me, one of which was that I wasn't feeling relieved at the end of meditation. But the problem was that my expectations for meditation were wrong. I expected to be relieved. But the true goal was understanding. Relief follows understanding. And that understanding is achieved by first listening to oneself.

> So how do I meditate? I just sit in silence. Start with five minutes. Keep all your electronics and any other distractions away. And just listen to yourself. Listen to what your mind is telling you. You might have an overflow of negative thoughts when you start, which is great! Because now you are actually becoming aware of what your mind is telling you. Only when you've become aware will you be able to accept the thought and what it's causing you to feel— and then make a choice about it.
>
> For example, you've just started meditating, and the first thought that comes to your mind is of a person who mistreated you, and you get this sense of urgency and panic to do something about it. You have two choices here: Either you follow this thought and feeling and end up at *I'm never going to find love or I'm not worthy of love.* Or you can say to this thought and feeling *I see you. I accept that I am thinking and feeling you. And I understand that you are coming from my mind. But you are not who I am. You are not welcome as a permanent resident in my home. You are here*

because my mind is thinking you, because my heart is feeling
you, but you are not me. And I choose not to follow you.

IN CHAPTER THREE, the Forgiveness room, I discussed cutting the marionette cords that chain you to your pain. Silence in this instance is crucial, because it unifies you with yourself. It's you against all that's chaining you. If you try to unchain yourself without being in silence, your energy isn't fully focused on the act of cutting the cords. It's not fully focused on retrieving all that power back into yourself. This might sound like a silly example, but you know how when you're driving and you're trying to figure out your destination, you turn down the radio or you tell the passengers in your car to lower their voices so you can focus? It's not that the sounds are stopping you from driving—it's that they're taking away the energy you want to put toward figuring out where you're headed. It's the same thing here. It's not the noise that hinders your task, but rather the resulting drain on your energy—energy that needs to be allocated toward the task at hand: your healing.

STEP 1: Sit in silence.

STEP 2: Close your eyes or focus on one object.

STEP 3: Imagine a person who hurt you. Think of all the power you're giving them, as represented by the cords that tie you (the marionette) to them. Each cord represents something you feel you can't let go of when it comes to that pain or that person.

STEP 4: Imagine picking up a pair of scissors. The scissors come directly from the foundation of your home. One blade is self-acceptance and one blade is self-awareness. You take the scissors to each cord separately and say *I accept you and I release you. You have no power over me.*

STEP 5: Every time you cut a cord, imagine its power flowing back into you. Into your heart. Into your home.

This activity is like saying *I'm dismantling your power over me. The power I thought was yours is now mine.*

IN CHAPTER FOUR, the Compassion room, I spoke about how I chose silence when I was struggling:

> Even though I was aching to speak to someone about what I was going through, my first instinct was to tell myself *They won't understand. So I'd better stay quiet. They'll ask me why I didn't come to them any sooner. But before that, they'll say something that will make me question myself . . . how could I not have known any better?*

That "first instinct" I'm referring to was my ego. It was my *Why can't I have that?* story. It was the voice that stopped me from opening up and raising my voice because that voice showed me the ending before I'd even begun. Without recognition of what was standing in the way of seeking the support I needed from those around me, I wouldn't have gotten to the point where I could differentiate between opening up in general and opening up to the right people—those who'd earned the right to hear my story. I wouldn't have learned that instead of isolating myself and keeping myself hidden, all I needed to do was to draw boundaries around my home.

IN CHAPTER FIVE, the Clarity room, I spoke about how I didn't listen to my gut when it told me to run.

> If something doesn't feel right in a way you can't explain, it probably isn't right. It's your body telling you something is off. I want you to listen to your gut. Whether or not you go with it isn't the issue. This is about not ignoring that it's trying to tell you something. To know what it's trying to tell you, you'll need to go inward.
>
> Throughout my situationship with Noah, I always felt something was wrong. I just didn't listen to my gut. I hoped it was wrong. I mistook the highs and lows of the confusion for liking him.
>
> Had I listened to my gut, which was telling me *This is not right. This doesn't feel right or healthy at all*, I would have saved myself so much grief.

The gut I'm referring to here was my logic. My knowing there were inconsistencies in Noah's behavior. It wasn't just a feeling. It wasn't my ego. It was my logic saying *Something doesn't add up*.

IN CHAPTER SIX, the Surrender room, I spoke about allowing yourself to experience the emotion that's standing at your door.

> Surrender . . . surrender to yourself. To what's really going on inside. Drop the mask. Drop the excuses. Drop the resistance. Drop the need to look like you're doing well by whatever standards there are around you. Your family, your community, the world, social media, and so on. This is why the tools in this room are called "submissions," not with the weak connotation, but with the opposite-of-resistance connotation.
>
> Just surrender. Don't just hear your inner voice. Actually *listen to* yourself. Listen to your heart. Hear your soul. And . . .
>
> Listen to your pain.
>
> Listen to your self.

IN CHAPTER SEVEN, "The Dream Garden," I spoke about listening to yourself.

When you start tuning in to yourself, thoughts will start presenting themselves to you. Here is a series of steps that will guide you as you listen to yourself:

1. Sit in silence.

2. Start noticing the variety of thoughts/emotions/voices that come to you.

3. Once you start identifying each one, ask yourself:

   a. What is the thought/emotion/voice telling me?

   b. Where is this thought/emotion/voice stemming from? (People's opinions, your ego, social constructs, and the like)

   c. Is this thought/emotion/voice true? (The answer should always be according to your authentic self.)

      i. If it is true, am I okay with it? If I'm not okay with it, what can I do to change it?

      ii. If it's not true, I will let my authentic voice speak back to it.

Listening to myself and identifying the voices within me transformed those voices from being rigid beliefs about myself to guiding lights toward understanding myself. That has brought me so much healing. I urge you when you read this book again to notice how you can use the process of listening to yourself to immensely change your understanding of yourself and the world around you.

NINE

Adapting to Your New Reality

You made it.

You've built your own home.

Or maybe you're still under construction. And that's okay.

Wherever you are in your journey of healing and making your way back to yourself, you are at your own unique stage of building your home. And how beautiful is that? You've taken ownership over your healing. You've decided to do what's right for you, not what anyone tells you you should do. Remember, before you decide where you're headed, you have to figure out where you actually are. You can't skip steps. The sooner you come to terms with that, the more effective your journey of healing will be.

So maybe you had to build your home from scratch. Maybe you had to construct your road to it with a few obstacles along the way. Maybe your foundation is still under construction. Maybe you've built a home and now it's time to move in. Maybe you've been living in someone else's home and it's time to move out. Maybe you've been homeless for a while and you're learning to adapt to living in a home. And maybe you already had a home within you and realized it needed renovations. Maybe you decided to move your furniture around for a fresh perspective. The *maybes* are endless.

Whatever stage you're at, healing means you are under construction. Your at-home self is under construction. And you need to honor the stage you're at. Don't be hard on yourself because of the pace you're moving at relative to the pace you believe you should be moving at. Healing is hard. And it takes time. It takes real change.

But do you know the one thing that will never change? The fact that you've taken that step to build your own home. The fact that you've taken the time to reflect on your homelessness all those years. The fact you've become aware of all that's standing in the way of you building your own home within yourself.

You've already accomplished the hardest part. So keep building. Keep working on yourself.

Yes, you may need to ask for help in building this home, but remember to welcome only those whose footsteps in your home are taken with compassion. Don't ask for help from those whose doors you so desperately knocked on in the past to welcome you. It's time for you to knock on your own door. It's time for you to welcome yourself.

While your home is under construction, you'll be experiencing many changes. Like a caterpillar becoming a butterfly, you are turning all you already are into a beautiful masterpiece; and that masterpiece is you. Fully you. At-home you.

> *You were always a masterpiece.*
> *The difference now*

is that your pieces
found more beauty in being
together
than in being scattered.
The difference now
is that you
are the master
of your pieces.

And beware of this: Expect that people from your past will knock at your door asking where the old you, the you that they know, is. When this happens, say:

She doesn't live here anymore (change the pronouns as they suit you). The old me stayed behind . . . somewhere far away that I will never visit again. The new me left parts of her old self in every person she built a home inside of. In every identity she defined herself by. She left her old self in every place that didn't value her. In every place that made her feel that being herself is too much or too undesirable.

And if they tell you anything that indicates that you owe them an explanation, say this:

I already grieved my past self. I honor her. I honor everything she taught me about my present self. My future self. My worth. My being. My value. You can grieve her, too, in your own way. I honor all the parts of her she placed in others, thinking she was building a home for herself in them. It was hard enough for me to learn how to grieve my past self on my own. My present job is not to help anyone grieve her. My job is not to explain or justify my change, my growth, and my transformation to anyone.

Does a butterfly explain
to the flowers
or the trees
or the sky
why she is no longer in her cocoon?
Do you not see
how beautiful my wings are?
I will not reverse my growth
to shrink into a smaller version of myself
that will fit into the cocoon
that I broke myself to break out of.

And if I knocked on your door during those times and you didn't open the door, know that I will never knock again. I am knocking on my own door right now. I might meet you somewhere every once in a while. I might invite you over at times, but you will enter with compassion. And I might decide to never welcome you again. And that's totally my right.

When you finish the building of your home, it's time to adapt to your new reality. Even if you're still under construction, it's time to adapt to your new reality. You are no longer a nomad. You are no longer sprinkling parts of you in other people or places or ideas just to feel like you belong. This home of yours ensures you are at home wherever you go. It doesn't matter where you are in the world or who is around you, you don't feel like an outcast. You feel that way only when you're not accepted. Now that you accept yourself, you fit in. You fit in your own life. How magnificent is that?

Wherever you go and whoever you're with, you carry your home within you. You don't look for a place to stay. You don't extend your roots to wherever the feeling of home comes from, because your home is here—inside of you. The search is over. You're here.

As you walk through the halls of your home, as you make your way from room to room, you will breathe in the scent of serenity. You're in a place of tranquility. A state of calm. A state of peace. Because even when you're dealing with the hardest situations in your life, you understand that the answer is within you. Not anywhere else. Not inside of anyone else. You understand that your circumstances don't define you—you define you. You are fully aware that your responsibility is to do what you can and let go of what is out of your control.

And, remember, just because you've built your own home, it doesn't mean the work is done. Just as you have to keep your physical place of living clean, tidy, and organized, you have to do the same within your home. Just as you have to fix something that breaks from time to time, reorganize a space, redecorate a room, or paint a fresh new color, you also have to do the same in your home. Just as you have to renovate your house from time to time, you have to do the same in your home. You may have to repurpose a room or add one based on what you need.

This is your home. Taking care of it is taking care of yourself. Upkeeping it is upkeeping yourself. Honoring it is honoring yourself.

Your home is your number one priority. You are your number one priority.

You might have setbacks. There might be days where you feel like you've abandoned yourself. You might hit the roadblock of not spending enough time in your home. You might even hit the roadblock of finding comfort in someone else's home. And that's okay. We all sometimes behave in a way that renders us feeling like we've betrayed ourselves. And that's because of the patterns that were ingrained in us. Don't be hard on yourself. A day in a state of not being at home with yourself doesn't mean you've lost your home. It just means you have to come back to yourself. But since you've done the big Welcome Home—you've taken the time to build that home—coming home will be easier, because now you know the road that leads to it. You know the way home. And you've already built a strong foundation for that home.

I want to take you with me to a moment of home. Walk with me.

Do you ever look at something you've seen before and notice something completely new about it? Or watch a movie you've watched before and notice a scene that you can now *see*? Because it hit you differently? One day I found myself looking through all the journals I'd filled over the years. Flipping through the pages, I could clearly see the pain that wove my words. I always saw that pain. But this time, that's not what popped out at me. This time, I saw past the pain. I saw the search. The search for something. The pull toward something that, all those years, I'd masked by an urge to behave a certain way, to speak a certain way, to react a certain way, to . . . be a certain way.

But the search. The search. What was I searching for?

I know now that back then I was searching for home. But what was the missing piece about that home?

Upon reading more and more. And more . . . the answer came to me, quickly, slowly, and peacefully all at the same time.

What's the missing piece?

And a whisper in my heart said: *Home* is you.

Home *is* you.

Not who your mind tells you you are, or who your mind tells you you're not. Not your past pains and what they've caused you to be, or what they've caused you to believe you need to be. That's not you. That's not home. Home is you, now—exclusive of all that. Because when you attach yourself to any of that, you've built your home in the past or the future.

Imagine yourself as an ocean. Home is the deep place in the ocean that nothing happening on the surface can affect. It's your inner, authentic self. Not the self at the surface that's affected by whatever current circumstances you're going through, or by past or future ones. That authentic you is always there, and it's always you. And it doesn't carry labels—someone who went through something, or someone who is about to go through something, or someone who is a label—it's just you.

When I finally came to that realization, it was the most humbling feeling I could ever have. It was humbling and freeing and empowering. It fully allowed me to embrace that inner self of mine. Not Najwa, not the writer, not the author, not the speaker, not the one who's writing books. Not the Najwa who has a certain face or a certain body or a certain age. Not the Najwa who's considered brave by many and cowardly by many. Not the Najwa who's in search of a home. And at the same time, not the Najwa who carried her home in her backpack, not the Najwa who was let down, or let go, or hurt . . . I wasn't her. I was . . . just me . . . now. And I felt like, yes, I've obviously known for a while that I'm whole, but now I *feel* whole. And the weird thing is I feel whole with a lot less than I've ever had, and a lot less than I ever thought I needed to have to feel whole.

> *I am the land my home is built on.*
> *I am my own home.*
> *And home is me.*
> *And to you, I am telling you:*
> *You are the land your home needs to be built on.*
> *You are your own home.*
> *Home is you.*
> *How light do you feel now? How free do you feel now?*
> *The weight of all you've been carrying has been so heavy,*
>   *hasn't it?*
> *It's been a while since you could breathe this fresh air,*
>   *hasn't it?*
> *It's been a while since you could feel this in touch with the*
>   *essence of who you truly are, hasn't it?*
> *That's over now.*
> *You've come back to yourself.*
> *Welcome home.*

Appendix: What Room(s) Would You Add?

Your healing journey is unique. Your way back to yourself is constructed by you—by how far back you had to go, by the unique obstacles you had to recognize and walk through. Building your own home reflects that uniqueness.

Your home will not be identical to anyone else's home, because you are the builder. You are the architect. You are the decorator. You are the chooser of where everything goes.

Are there any additional rooms you'd like to have in your home?

For each room you decide to add:

What would you call this room?

What is the purpose of this room?

When do you enter this room?

For example:

When I'm feeling . . . a certain way.

When I'm thinking . . . a certain way.

How do you anticipate feeling as you leave this room?
For example:

> You feel less confused/more clear as you leave the Clarity room.

> You feel less resistant/more open to experiencing an emotion as you leave the Surrender room.

What pillars would it stand on? Remember that the pillars are the rules or essentials that support the room. You can choose not to call them pillars, just as I called them lanterns in the Dream Garden (Chapter Seven). Be creative!

What would the furniture (strategies and tools) in this room be? Remember that the furniture is made up of the strategies that will serve the purpose of this room.

What would you call the furniture?

For example, strategies in the Forgiveness room were outlets; in the Clarity room, mirrors; in the Surrender room, submissions.

You can name them whatever fits your needs. Again, be creative! This is YOUR home. Fill it up and decorate it as you wish!

If I could add a room, it would be the Writing room. And its purpose would be to serve as a safe space for me to write all my thoughts and feelings on paper.

There would only be one pillar: *Write it out as it is.*

I include some of those writings here. You may choose to put some of these as canvases on the wall in the hallways of your home. I also include, where applicable, suggestions about where to place them.

SIX BOXES, ONE MOMENT
June 15, 2017

Picture this:

I am standing within the outline of a box marked with tape on the ground. Right next to me, within my box, are educators from several schools. In the box across from me, students from another school. In the box next to them, students from another school. It goes on and on. Six boxes. Six different groups. I am the only woman with a head covering in all six groups.

The idea is for us to realize that we have more in common than we realize. We are asked to walk up to the front if certain phrases apply to us. For example, those who like pineapple on their pizza.

A few prompts go by.

Now comes: *If you identify as LGBT2Q+, come up to the front.* A few students and staff walk up to the front.

Then comes: . . . *and those who are allies.* I start walking to the front and I notice this: the seven students with me, who all identify as Muslim, are all walking up to the front. Every single one of them. I feel so proud.

You might think this is the moment I'm writing about. It's not.

When we return to our boxes, a girl from the opposite box looks at me. Once she catches my attention, she smiles, which seems in the moment the biggest smile I've ever seen. I smiled and looked away, then it hit me it was more than that. I looked back. She smiled at me again. It was as if she'd made a realization. I saw change in this student's eyes. This endearing moment reminded me of the power of leading through action, not just words. This student had clearly been affected somehow, in a positive way, by my choice to walk up as an ally when Muslims are often portrayed as haters or judgmental of the LGBT2Q+ community. I saw a wall, a barrier to understanding, crumbling right before my eyes.

On my drive home, I kept telling myself that it couldn't have been so powerful. Maybe I was just overthinking. But the power of that moment would not leave me until I found myself writing this.

May we always be open to these walls breaking and to these bridges being built.

BLACK LIVES MATTER
2015

Peel my skin
and a few more layers.
Rip through my flesh
and grind it to pieces.
Will you not find
a heart like yours?
Will you not find
blood running through my veins
like yours?
Will you not find lungs
struggling for air
like yours?
Tell me, was I born with an organ called
violence?
Did the color of skin I was born with

tattoo danger all over me?
What gives you the right
to strip me of my humanity?
What gives you the right
to take away the life
that you did not give to me?
Did the color of your skin make
you more worthy of life
than me?
No, sir.
You keep your life and
let me keep mine.
I only want my heart to beat out of my chest
out of love,
not fear of your gun.

YOU'LL NEVER GO BACK TO THE PERSON YOU WERE BEFORE
January 3, 2018

You'll never go back to the person you were before. It's impossible. Believe me, I tried it myself. And while I'm on that note, it's impossible to be loved, believed, or respected by everyone. People who don't even know you will pretend to know you and make judgments about you. But don't let that get to you. It's a reflection of who they are, not who YOU are.

It used to bother me when someone didn't see me for who I really was. I felt the need to explain myself. But not anymore. I'm realizing day by day that the way that people see me is out of my control. And that the way I see myself is more important than the way others see me. No one walked in my shoes. So no one has the right to tell me what path I walked or how marred I was.

In July, I wrote this piece about abuse. Today, when I read it, I cried. Not because I felt it. But because I realized how far I'd come from that place. This is what I wrote: "It's like someone stripping your soul out of your body bit by bit, with pleasure, stepping all over it, ripping it into pieces, and telling you to do the same. Then they stuff all that brokenness back into you and tell you you are broken. Something is wrong with you. And you're crazy for even believing that someone as crazy as you is worthy of being heard. You start to scream, but they pretend not to hear you. And they tell you no one else will hear you either. You ask them why they did what they did to you, and they pretend like they have no idea what you're talking about. And they tell you that no one will know what you're talking about either, so you better stay quiet. It's like trusting someone until they get you to the middle of the ocean, then being thrown in the water when you don't know how to swim. So you start to drown. In an ocean of self-hate and self-blame, gasping for any raft of sanity. And every time you put your head up to ask for help, they push you back into the water. Until you surrender. And become blue. There's a little force inside of you that takes you back to the surface, but you get there only sometimes. If you're lucky. So when you do, you beg them to help you get out. But they don't. Then they tell everyone around to look at you and how worthless you are. How could you get into the ocean when you don't know how to swim?"

Today, I'm out of that ocean. And I'm no longer blue. I'm no longer begging anyone to help me or get me out of the water. I got out on my own. And I no longer feel the need to pretend I'm okay if I really am not. I'm healing. And I need to honor that. I'm learning to respect what my body tells me. What my heart tells me. And what my soul tells me. And I'm seeing myself as the me that I know now more than ever.

YOU ARE NOT MY OPPRESSOR

March 11, 2017

You are not my oppressor.
You are not my ruler.
If speaking the truth makes me a tyrant,
then let me be a tyrant.
If resisting your executive orders makes me a rebel,
then I wish to revolt.
I wish to defy.
I wish to say NO.
If standing in the way of your pipelines makes me an outlaw,
then put your pipeline right through me
because I will not
move out of your way.
And if you build a wall in my face,
I will climb it.
Let it reach the seventh sky,
I will shatter it.
Brick. By. Brick.
And it. Will. Crumble.
Just like your ego that is hanging by a thread,

your wall is built on sand that is quicker than the hail of a storm.
And if you turn me away because of my
color, because of my
beliefs, or my identity.
Then turn me away.
But don't you think for a second that
pushing me away clears your slate.
If you push me away because I am seeking peace
and safety,
then you have taken part in killing me.
Does it surprise you that a woman like me is speaking to you the
*   way that I am?*
Let me remind you that what's wrapped around my head
is not wrapped around my mouth.
So I will not allow the label that you wrap me with
to wrap around my voice.
If the truth hurts you,
that's your problem.
You may ignore it, but
don't you dare change it to "alternative facts."
The voice of justice will remain
louder
than corruption.
Your corruption, sir, has turned us into
corruptors.
Your oppression, sir,
has changed us into oppressors.
But your coldness
has ignited the warmth of humanity with us.

So . . . as a human, I remind you
that strength does not come from gaining power and control.
Strength does not come from building walls
or hiding behind forts and bans.
Strength comes from being
human.
And as a woman, I tell you:
Take your eyes off of my body.
That's not where my glory lies.
Stop telling me that my heart makes me weak.
My heart makes the world beat.
Stop telling me that
"boys will be boys" and that it is my fault
if you cannot control yourself around me.
I do not accept less than
"Humans will be humans."

CULTIVATING EMPATHY IN STUDENTS

March 17, 2017

As I sat in a meeting with my colleagues to discuss creating a positive school culture for learning, we all enriched the discussion by sharing our stories and experiences. By the end, it seemed we were all coming back to the same point: empathy.

So I started reflecting: Are we born with empathy? Or is it something we need to develop? And, if we are born with empathy, what happens over the years? How do we lose it? Why do some people seem to be naturally empathetic, while others have to put in the extra effort to really understand what someone else is going through? If I could answer these questions, I would be able to assess and decipher what our role as educators is when it comes to empathy. Do we teach it from scratch? Do we nourish it? Do we open opportunities in class for it to be shared? What do we *really* do?

Let's take a moment here while I reflect on my own self. I've struggled my whole life with being too emotionally invested in anything. Yes, anything that spurs any kind of emotion. Instead of having to actively remind myself to be empathetic, I have been taught by my environment to always be conscious of not being *too* empathetic. It wasn't until the last few years of my life that I've learned to cherish this attribute within me. It didn't happen overnight. There were many turning points along the way, such as the one I am about to describe.

I think back to this memory with one of the Syrian newcomers I had the honor of working with, which I wrote about in the past.

As we work on making cubes with the six universal emotions on all six sides, my high school students and I are talking about the importance of expressing ourselves and our emotions. One of my students looks at his peer's cube and, with the biggest smile on his face, says: "That's so colorful! Did you dip it into a paint can or something?!" My group of about ten students bursts into laughter. The volunteer in my classroom turns to this student and says: "You are so funny!" I, at this point, am just translating back and forth. He says: "Is that a good thing?" She says: "Of course! You always make this environment so happy!" He turns to me and says: "I never used to be like this, but one day, my cousin told me, when you die, what will you take with you? Not the sadness. Not the misery. You will only take the happiness and goodness that you spread."

At this point, I am so proud and shocked with the level of maturity that this teen demonstrated.

"Then my cousin died," he says.

How would you react in this kind of situation? Do you ask questions? Do you worry about the rest of the students in the class listening to this? Do you change the topic? Do you ignore what you just heard? . . . What do you do?

I decided to take off the armor that I had on and to allow my vulnerability to do its work at this point. If this student opened up the topic, that means he already trusted me with it. So, little by little, he unpacked his story right before me, and I could see it so clearly as he described it in the gravest possible detail. It got worse. I resisted stopping him from talking many, many times.

It was difficult to listen to. It was difficult to take it all in. But, if it was difficult for me to listen to, how difficult was it for him to go through it and talk about it?

That was one of the defining moments of my teaching career, because when I went home, I reflected deeply on my role as a teacher. I couldn't stop the human in me from affecting the teacher in me. My role is to ensure a safe learning environment, and that sometimes could lead to wanting to shelter students from the pain of the world. But how could the pain go away if it's not acknowledged? Perhaps my role is to create not just a safe learning environment, but also a resilient one. An empowering one. That's when I realized that both the human and the teacher in me are one. You cannot be one without the other.

So on this recent journey to research whether empathy is inborn or developed over the years, sure enough, I discovered that it is *inborn* but must be nurtured over the years. Nurturing it begins with acknowledging its presence in the first place. What does that *really* mean? It means we must be more attentive to the natural ways in which our children demonstrate empathy, kindness, and compassion. And we must reward these demonstrations. A reward could be as simple as saying "Thank you for your kindness." Never dismiss someone's natural ability to be empathetic, kind, or compassionate. Over time, such dismissal can silence and deafen this natural gift we're all born with.

Now, you might be wondering why I chose "*Cultivating* Empathy" for the title of this piece. It's simple. *Cultivating* means *fostering the growth of* something. In other words, we're acknowledging that empathy already exists within us. All we need to do is create the proper conditions for it to be active and alive. When we plan our lessons, we are told to start with students' prior knowledge. This should also apply to how we educate the humans in our students. We need to start with what they already have, and with what they know about what they already have. That's how we set them up for success. That's how we strengthen their strengths and empower them to have the courage to be the humans they already are. More important, we should never *assume* that students know how they should act or react, because we don't know what their home and social environments have conditioned them to believe. When we assume, we are more likely to judge. And when we judge, we are more likely to give negative consequences to students when they genuinely might not know any better. When we have a certain standard, we might miss a simple gesture of empathy on behalf of a student. We must therefore be attentive and not shy away from acknowledging these gestures, as simple as they may be.

Based on this knowledge, how will you use the empathy that already exists within you to cultivate, *to foster the growth of,* empathy in your students? Will you allow the human in you to enrich the teacher in you?

TO MY FUTURE DAUGHTER
2013

There will always be someone who will tell you that you're not good enough, pretty enough, or unique enough.

There will always be someone who will tell you that you're only as beautiful as your face and your body.

There will always be someone who will tell you that your worth depends on how much attention you can get.

There will always be someone who will tell you that your education is a waste.

But I will always be there to tell you this . . .

The beauty within you cannot be compared to anyone else's.

You are unique because the moment you came to this life, you brought a whole new kind of beauty. A whole new kind of innocence. A whole new kind of ability to make people love. You define beauty. Beauty does not define you. To your parents, you are the most beautiful and precious human in existence. Never forget that. Never doubt that. As you grow, society will push you to conform to the ideals it creates. Those ideals will always change, but who you are should never change to anything but the better.

A pretty face may get you attention, but a pretty heart will get you respect. A pretty face may get you popularity, but a beautiful, reasonable mind will get you true happiness that lasts a lifetime. Your attitude may get you attention, but kindness will get you genuine love. True love is not easily found, because things that last a lifetime are rare. You are rare, and that's a fact. Don't ever allow anyone to make you doubt that. Those are the people you need to remove from your life.

Close your eyes and think of those who acknowledge your goodness and your authenticity. Look to those who look out for you. You really must believe that if you ever feel down, there is always someone out there who feels the same way. And that unless you learn to see yourself for who you are on the inside, you'll always be a prisoner of what those around you think of you.

That jail is more torturous than any other. Real flaws are not those you have on the outside, but those hidden in your heart, in your mind, in your soul. Work on fixing them first. The more you focus on your inside, the more beautiful, confident, and independent your outside will be.

Your education is what makes you a queen, because it crowns your heart with the ability to make a difference in this world.

Independence will be your guard from every power that tries to weaken you or defeat you. Some will try to convince you that independence scares people away. That's true. It will scare the wrong people away and will make those who are right for you respect you more, love you more, and value you more.

My little girl, if I still haven't convinced you that beauty is about goodness, kindness, honesty, humbleness, and understanding. . . . If I still haven't convinced you that beauty is that of the soul, the heart, and the mind, then think of your mother's face. Think of every wrinkle on it. Think of every story behind each one. Think of every sacrifice made behind each one. Think of every second she could have chosen to focus on herself but instead consciously and willingly decided to focus on you and your future. Isn't she the most beautiful woman on earth?

CANVASES FOR YOUR HOME

DON'T LOSE YOURSELF. Often we come across people who are lost. They overwhelm our hearts with the need to help them come out of their darkness. And that's not wrong. To want to help someone is not wrong. The mistake begins when you consume yourself with their darkness and forget about yourself. There must be a balance. Never allow yourself to lose yourself as you try to help someone find themselves. If it happens, learn from it, and move past it. It's not your responsibility to save anyone. You may help, yes. But do not save someone by making yourself in need of saving.

Suggested use: On the door of the Compassion room or inside of it.

SEE YOURSELF. If they fail to see you during the darkness, a thousand suns shining your way won't make them see you. Our hearts adapt to the darkness just like our eyes do. If their heart wants to see you, it will. And if it doesn't, you have the power to let your heart shine elsewhere. You really do.

Suggested use: On the door of the Compassion room or inside of it.

BE GRATEFUL. Don't ask for happiness to come your way. Rather, ask for eyes and a heart that see happiness in what you already have and in the simplest of things around you. Ask for health, for simplicity, for ease of mind. Ask for fewer things but more quality. Ask for goodness. Ask for contentment and conviction in your beliefs and in your condition. Ask for the motivation to pursue your dreams, and for less weakness in your emotions. Ask for a balance between your mind's logic and your heart's reason. Most important, ask for the power to want to change to the better every moment you're blessed to be able to breathe comfortably, because millions out there breathe only because they must strive to survive. You're more than just surviving. So live. Give as much as you can, while you can, and be happy.

Suggested use: On the door of the Self-Love room or inside it.

WALK AWAY. Have the courage to walk away from the stories you don't belong in. Don't settle for being a secondary character when you deserve to be the main one. People change, and that's okay. But don't change yourself to fit their standards. You may find yourself slowly drifting out of a plot, but that doesn't mean that you were never part of the main events. You may find your importance slowly fading, but that doesn't mean you were never the focus. Don't regret doing your best to keep what you had. It shows your loyalty. Don't regret giving all you can. It shows your commitment. But should you find yourself disrespected or unappreciated, don't be afraid to put an end to your existence in their story. Walk away with pride, knowing that you put your heart into what you loved. Never settle for just existing. The world is full of stories. Create your own.

Suggested use: On the door of the Surrender room or inside of it.

TAKE THE RISK. Some decisions in life are more important than others. And some require risks that are greater than others. But we always want someone to tell us that we are going to be okay, that wherever we get to is going to be great, better than where we are right now. But the thing is, you can never get that assurance, because you never know what the future holds. Yes, you might be afraid of letting go of the place you're in, because you're afraid of not getting to a better place. But if you stay in your spot, you might regret one day not trying to get to wherever you'd like to be. You might regret not moving from your spot. If you get to a new destination that's not what you hoped for, at least you will have tried. At least you will have ventured. At least you will have learned new lessons, met new people, and learned new ways of thinking of things. You never know what trying could get you to, so if you're contemplating a risk and it's important enough to you, go ahead and go for it.

Suggested use: At the entrance to the Dream Garden or inside of it.

GIVE YOURSELF VALIDATION. Don't base your self-worth on what those who broke you have to say about you. Why do you still believe them anyway? Be careful whose voice you allow into your head. The person you trusted with your heart, who shattered it to pieces, isn't worthy of anything more than your forgiveness. You don't need anyone's approval to be yourself. You don't need anyone's permission to be yourself. And you don't need anyone's love to heal you. You own yourself. So define yourself. Approve of yourself. Give yourself permission to be yourself. Love yourself before you seek love from anyone. And you will heal.

Suggested use: On the door of the Forgiveness room or inside of it.

SIT WITH THE PAIN. One of the hardest things in life must be getting over the pain of being wrongfully treated, with or without an apology. An apology alone will not take the pain away. And when you do forgive that person, forgiveness does not take the pain away nor does it heal you instantly. Don't depend on the person who inflicted pain upon you to wake up and realize they need to take it away. Even if they acknowledge your pain, it still won't take it away. It won't erase it, because time can't be turned back. So stop giving those who hurt you so much power over your healing and your moving on. In due time, you will forgive them. When you're ready, you'll know. But for now, you must feel the pain, and let it leave you. You are in charge only of yourself. You can only control yourself. So take control over your pain and turn it into strength.

Suggested use: On the door of the Forgiveness room or inside of it.

WHERE WOULD YOU ADD the canvases that follow?

CONTROL YOURSELF. When you dwell on things you can't change, those things gain control of you. So instead of saying *This person is lying to me—I want them to be honest.* Or *This person said they care about me, but they don't—I want them to care about me.* Or *This person was insincere with me—I want them to be sincere* . . . Instead of saying those things, say *All I can do is be sincere with them. All I can do is be honest with them. All I can do is care about them.*

Instead of focusing on changing them, focus on making yourself a better person. And when the day comes that the people who are meant to be in your life come into your life, you'll be so thankful you spent your time making yourself a better person rather than trying to make other people better when you have no control over them.

STOP COMPARING. Stop comparing your life to anyone else's life. If others have something you want, go after it and achieve it, but don't make your focus being better than them. Even worse, don't make your focus *being* them. Don't let this home you're building within yourself for yourself be a place that doesn't resemble you: one that you picked from brochures and magazines showing homes that you wished your home looked like. Don't let happiness be so far away from who you are. It's available to you now, as you are.

True liberation is not when you're able to pretend you don't care, but when you actually don't care. Stop focusing your healing on how others view it. Focus your healing on you actually healing.

WHICH CANVASES WOULD YOU ADD? And where in your home would you place them?

Acknowledgments

This journey would not have been possible without the following people who held my hand and lit the road to *Welcome Home.*

Thank you,

Mom: for teaching me kindness.

Dad: for teaching me integrity.

My siblings: for carrying me on your shoulders.

My partner in life and love: for endlessly chasing the sun with me.

Katie: for your loyalty, commitment, advocacy, and caring presence.

Marc: for believing in me and my writing from day one. And for cheering on the hint of Kanye in me.

Tess: for your kindness and unbridled commitment to advocate for me.

Marc and Tess: for listening to me talk about an idea I've had for years, looking at each other, then at me, and saying, "That's the book you need to write!"

Donna: for walking with me every step of the way to make *Welcome Home* the masterpiece it is today.

The team at Penguin Random House: for helping me build homes all over the world.

My friends (you know who you are): for being love and light. For reminding me of who I am when I forget.

Sammy Roach: for transforming my thoughts into beautiful illustrations.

Phillip Millar: for taking the law a hundred steps further and empowering me to raise my voice as loud as I need to.

My loyal audience: for walking this journey with a lost soul coming home to herself.

Index

About the Author

Najwa Zebian is a Lebanese Canadian activist, author, speaker, and educator. Her search for a home was central to her early years as she struggled to find her place in the world. She became a teacher and a doctoral candidate in educational leadership. As Najwa began to write in an effort to connect with and heal her first students, a group of young refugees, she found that she was also writing to heal herself. The author of three collections of poetry, she delivered the TEDx talk "Finding Home Through Poetry" and recently launched a digital school, Soul Academy, and a podcast, *Stories of the Soul*. Her work has been featured in the *New York Times*, *Glamour*, *Elle Canada*, *HuffPost*, and more.

For more inspiration, pick up this keepsake treasury of Najwa's most beloved poetry and short prose.

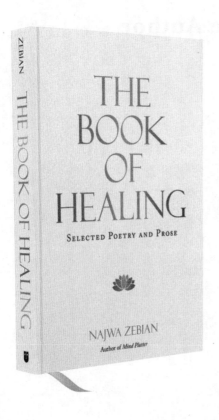

Powerful and moving, *The Book of Healing* is a curated selection of personal favorites from Najwa Zebian's three bestselling books—*Mind Platter*, *The Nectar of Pain*, and *Sparks of Phoenix*. This gift-worthy volume offers heartfelt reflections on letting go, discovering self-worth, and cultivating resilience.

Available wherever books are sold.